The Civil War in
FAIRFAX COUNTY

The Civil War in
FAIRFAX COUNTY

★ ★ ★ ★ ★ ★ ★ ★ ★ ★ ★ ★ ★

CIVILIANS AND SOLDIERS

Charles V. Mauro

Charleston   London

THE
History
PRESS

Published by The History Press
Charleston, SC 29403
www.historypress.net

Cover image: The courthouse at Fairfax in Union hands showing both civilians and soldiers, 1863. *Fairfax County Public Library, Photographic Archives.*

First published 2006
Second printing 2008
Third printing 2008
Manufactured in the United States

ISBN 978.1.59629.148.5

Library of Congress Cataloging-in-Publication Data
Mauro, Charles V.
  The Civil War in Fairfax County : civilians and soldiers / Charles V.
Mauro.
     p. cm.
  Includes bibliographical references and index.
  ISBN-13: 978-1-59629-148-5 (alk. paper)
  ISBN-10: 1-59629-148-6 (alk. paper)
 1. Fairfax County (Va.)--History, Military--19th century. 2. Fairfax
County (Va.)--Social conditions--19th century. 3. Fairfax County
(Va.)--History, Local. 4. Virginia--History--Civil War, 1861-1865--Social
aspects. 5. United States--History--Civil War, 1861-1865--Social aspects.
6. Battles--Virginia--Fairfax County--History--19th century. 7.
Virginia--History--Civil War, 1861-1865--Campaigns. 8. United
States--History--Civil War, 1861-1865--Campaigns. I. Title.

 F232.F2M3 2006
 973.7'55--dc22

                        2006025843

CONTENTS

ACKNOWLEDGEMENTS

My first note of appreciation goes to fellow authors Brad Gernand and Kim Holien for their encouragement and suggestions for material to use for this book when it was only a thought in my mind. Fellow authors Don Hakenson and Gregg Dudding also took their valuable time to point me in the right direction for reference material.

Beth Mitchell and Edith Sprouse have to be commended for their extraordinary effort in preparing the *Abstracts of Claims for Civil War Losses, Fairfax County* from the thousands of pages of the Southern Claims Commission documenting the lives and losses of the civilians in Fairfax County during the war.

Very special thanks to Suzanne Levy and Anita Ramos of the Virginia Room of the Fairfax City Regional Library for allowing me extra access to the *Abstracts*, the basic material upon which this book was written.

Thanks to Brian Conley of the Virginia Room for his knowledge and support in selecting the photographs for this book. Thanks to Kathy Hoffman and Linda Pierce, also of the Virginia Room, for their help in finding the maps to use to research this book. Thanks also to Tim Duskin, of the National Archives and Records Administration, who opened my eyes to the wealth of information stored there.

Thanks to Dan Woolley for the trip up the Potomac for the picture of Mount Vernon. Thanks to Lewis Leigh Jr. for the access to Laura Ratcliffe's album. Thanks also go to Steve Wolfsberger for his invaluable expertise in preparing the map presented in this book so that the readers have a chance to "see" where these events took place.

And as always, thanks to my wife, Nancy, who put up with me as I put this book together.

INTRODUCTION

Much, if not most, of what has been written about the American Civil War has been written about the campaigns, battles, generals, leaders or military aspects of the war. Very little is focused on the non-combatants—those who were also forced to survive under wartime conditions, those who where forced to flee their homes to avoid the danger to their lives, those whose property was destroyed or confiscated by the military forces around them—in short, the civilians. The effect of the war on the civilian population continued long after the fighting ceased. As Maris Vinovskis writes,

> *The survivors not only faced the inevitable problems of reentering civilian society; some undoubtedly continued to have vivid memories of the bloodiest war in the history of the United States. Memories of the war were shared by a large percentage of the entire population, as almost everyone had a loved one, close friend, or relative who fought in that conflict.*[1]

Southern civilians obviously suffered the predominant amount of property destruction. Both Northern and Southern civilians, however, endured the inflated prices of goods during the war and taxes that reduced the incomes they were able to earn. And even though the war generally stimulated economic growth in the North, recent studies have identified a decline in the "rate of industrializing, and the growth of per capita wealth" for those who lived in the North.[2]

What was civilian life like at the dawn of the Civil War? It is simply improper to assume today's values and lifestyles are the same as those civilians held over 140 years ago in a highly agrarian, community-centric culture. In antebellum society, livelihoods, lifestyles, government, customs, religious views and morals were significantly different than those in the twenty-first century.

For a start, Americans in the mid-nineteenth century lived their lives by strict individual ethics. Their daily personal lives often had an involvement in religious practices. One's belief in "good" and "evil" was tested daily and was absolute, not relative to the situation in question. "From infancy, mid-nineteenth century Americans were bombarded with moral teachings. Children were taught that right was right, and wrong was wrong, even if wrong was done for a good cause. Everlasting damnation was a compelling argument for long term goals with a view towards the afterlife and eternal future."[3]

Americans believed in divine intervention. Events in one's daily life, whether something good or bad happened, were attributable directly to God's or Satan's influence. For example, mid-nineteenth-century Americans "credited God with determining the success or failure of medical treatments, trusting that even a bad doctor could bring good health if God willed it."[4] If an accident befell some, it was the direct handiwork of Satan. During the war, this led soldiers to attribute their safety or to accept their possible deaths as the will of God rather than the actions of themselves and those around them.

In the agricultural society that existed at the time, having numerous children was seen as an asset to the family. Boys worked on the farm while girls provided domestic help. Widows and widowers often remarried a second or even a third time in order to keep the farm operating. Women had children as long as they were able in order to provide "labor" for the family farm. Families or family members could also count on employment with other family members in times of need. This sense of family led many fleeing in fear for their lives or having lost their property during the war to move to safer areas where they had blood ties more than willing to take them in.

A prewar agrarian society meant that "more Americans were involved in growing crops and raising animals than any other occupation." Most farmers followed in the footsteps of their fathers. The minority of men who were not involved in farming could be employed in trades such as farriers (shoeing horses), founders (casting metal or glass), drivers or engineers; or they were professionals who were lawyers, ministers, professors, bankers or representatives of the government. On the other hand, most women worked in the home, while a minority ran part-time or full-time businesses as milliners (designing or making hats), dressmakers or shop-women. The women who worked in their homes on the farm were highly valued partners in managing the household and teaching their children.[5]

Of course those who entered the military were part of this cross section of society: "99 percent of the men who fought in the war had been civilians before." Once the men had gone off to war, family members sent them a steady stream of letters, socks and supplies such as preserves or blankets. The longer the men were away, the greater the hardship on the families left behind. Women took greater roles in running the family farm or business and dealing with their finances. Many in the Southern states were eventually left destitute, struggling to survive, subject to the marauding soldiers (of both armies), seeing their meager foodstuffs and supplies dwindling and eventually dependent on others for their day-to-day existence.[6]

When the Civil War began, those civilians who did not become soldiers continued their occupations if they were able, but changed customers, from the private sector to the government. They worked to provide swords and cannons instead of working as silversmiths or making steam engine boilers. If the jobs were available, civilians worked directly for the wartime government constructing and repairing wagons, caissons and pontoon bridges. Women worked as seamstresses making military uniforms and even labored alongside men in ammunition factories. Both armies looked to their civilians to provide the goods they needed. Farmers also provided food for the armies, although as we shall see, much was simply confiscated, taken or stolen wherever the armies went with little or no remuneration.

Both governments also enlisted the help of civilians when doctors and nurses were in short supply to provide care in hospitals. Although this did not always involve direct medical assistance, some civilians "collected and distributed supplies and food, kept records, cleaned, and communicated with soldier's relatives and friends."[7]

For many civilians, their concern for—or the death of—a relative or close friend was the central event of the war. Few questioned their support of the North or the South early in the war. The prevailing wisdom was that the war would be short and those who left would soon return. Initial enthusiasm waned, however, as the casualties mounted and hope for a quick victory vanished.[8]

How did individual civilians live and react to the tumultuous events going on around them during the war? We do have a few diaries, which we can perhaps use to attribute the writers' views and reactions to the circumstances around them to the general population. A better source of information of life during the war would be the memoirs of a greater number of civilians rather than a few, but unfortunately that is not available. Although not published as such, the lives and conditions of quite a number of Civil War civilians were recorded after the war in the files of a government agency as a result of the appeals from thousands of civilians who had sustained losses during the Civil War.

Congress created the Southern Claims Commission in 1870 to address civilian claims for loss of personal property to the Union army in twelve Southern states during the war. Local commissions heard these claims and determined the authenticity of each one, deciding whether the claimant owned the property, the claimant saw the property taken by Union troops and whether the claimant was loyal to the Union during the war (determined by the claimant's own statements and corroborating testimony from other witnesses). The twelve states allowed to petition the government for their losses were Alabama, Arkansas, Florida, Georgia, Louisiana, Mississippi, North Carolina, South Carolina, Tennessee, Texas, Virginia and West Virginia. And as will be seen, many Southerners did not consider it lying to fib to a Yankee bureaucrat in order to receive compensation for their losses during the war.

As a result of this process, 22,298 claims made between 1871 and 1880 totaled $60.3 million. Almost one-third, 32 percent, actually proved both their loyalty and their losses, and although they received amounts far less than their individual claims, $4.6 million was actually paid by government checks to the claimants.

More importantly to us today, the claims processed by the commission created a fascinating paper trail from the claimants and from the people who testified for or against the claimants, providing a wealth of detail about the lives of the civilians as they faced the uncertainty of war on a daily basis. They faced problems not only from the battles and skirmishes that occurred on their very doorsteps, but also from the soldiers who came and took whatever food, wood, livestock and resources they needed from whoever happened to be in their way. These were the very same resources the civilians needed for their everyday existence.

Those civilians who fled their property knew full well it might not be there when they returned. Those who stayed to protect their property risked their lives in doing so, and some did indeed die in the process. Others did their best to appear neutral, knowing that with sentiments running exceedingly high, even their neighbors would turn them over to the authorities on the "other side" if they espoused their views in disagreement with others. Others had to deal with the knowledge that members of their own family held allegiances to both sides, causing untold family friction.

We look back on the Civil War now with the certainty of knowing its outcome, knowing what happened and knowing what was about to happen as we continually study the events that took place on the soil we live on today. The civilians who lived day to day through these events had no idea what was going to happen next. They lived with daily fear of what would directly threaten their property, their livelihoods, their family members and even their lives.

We can still visit the places today where these civilians lived, but we will never have the capability to know or to understand fully what it was like to live through four years of daily unpredictability. We can never imagine the daily strain and stress of having one's way of life changed, not knowing when the war would end, not knowing what the outcome would be for them after it ended or if they would even survive to see it played out. Only they can tell us their stories. Only they can try to impart to us what life and death were like in these times. Such are the stories of this book.

FAIRFAX COUNTY VIRGINIA

The naming of Virginia arose from Sir Walter Raleigh's attempt to establish a colony in Roanoke, North Carolina, in 1588. Virginia Dare was the first English baby born in the New World on August 18, 1587, named in honor of England's Queen Elizabeth I. Known as the "Virgin Queen" as she never married or had children, Elizabeth approved Raleigh's attempt to establish a colony for the riches it might bring the English. The colonists, however, disappeared and it was not until 1607 that the first successful colony was established, this time in Jamestown, Virginia, past Cape Henry at the opening of the Chesapeake Bay in southeastern Virginia. Looking for a crop to support their existence, a Jamestown colonist named John Rolfe learned to grow tobacco and the colonists shipped their first shipment to England ten years after Jamestown was founded. English demand and Virginia supply of this crop would subsequently affect the history of the colonies and lead to conditions for the Civil War.

Tobacco turned into the gold the colonists were seeking to profit from their lives in the Americas. With great demand but low prices in England, the colonists needed to grow increasingly large quantities of tobacco to make higher profits, and growing more tobacco required more land. Large tracts of land became the key to growing tobacco, which was the means to profit.[9]

In 1640 King Charles II of England granted all the land in Virginia north of the Rappahannock River to the Potomac River to seven Englishmen. By 1719, Thomas, Sixth Lord of Fairfax, gained control of this land, identified as the "Northern Neck" proprietary. In 1742, 12,588 acres in the Northern Neck were legally formed into Fairfax

County. Government was established, land grants were given out and speculators moved north from the Virginia Tidewater area. Among other crops, tobacco was grown and taken to warehouses along the Potomac River to be shipped to England, one warehouse in a town later named Alexandria in 1749 fulfilling the dreams of the English monarchy to gain wealth and riches from the colonies.[10]

The establishments of areas to later become towns in Fairfax County were developing even before the county was named. William Fitzhugh I was granted nearly 25,000 acres in 1685. Later named Ravensworth, this proprietary was centered in what would become Annandale. Thomas Lee took out a patent of 2,630 acres in 1719, an area that was later named Langley. The town of Dranesville in western Fairfax County emerged from a grant of 1,725 acres to James Thomas in 1727. Robert Carter, who would earn the nickname Robert "King Carter" for the enormous amounts of land he would acquire, obtained 30,000 acres in western Fairfax County between 1727 and 1729, including what would become Frying Pan and Herndon.[11]

Other areas had more humble beginnings. The city of Falls Church traces its earliest known single inhabitant to 1699. The property of Centreville's earliest known farmer was recorded in 1739, raising tobacco and rolling hogshead—round wooden casks—of tobacco along what were literally called "rolling" roads to the ports on the Potomac. By 1773, the area had grown enough to be known as the village of Newgate, which became the town of Centreville in 1792.

When Fairfax County was established in colonial Virginia, the county government was the "basic unit of local government." A courthouse and offices for the justices, clerk and lawyers were required to be built. Accordingly, a courthouse was built at Freedom Hill, just south and west of today's Tysons Corner, conveniently along the Alexandria-Leesburg Road, today's Leesburg Turnpike (or Route 7).[12]

However, as the population in Alexandria grew more rapidly than the population in the western portion of the county, the courthouse was subsequently moved to Alexandria by order of the governor in 1752. The courthouse remained in Alexandria until 1798 when, due to neglect and lack of maintenance, the Virginia General Assembly ordered the search for a new location, this time in the center of the county. In 1800 a new courthouse was built in the town of Providence nine miles west of Alexandria. Drawn by the new center of activity and aided by the construction of new roads to the courthouse, a new community developed in Providence, which also became known as Fairfax Court House.[13]

Fairfax County was developing and growing. An integral part of the growth and profit for the county's residents was its cash crop, tobacco. Growing tobacco profitably required land, transportation and labor. The land was available. Transportation, both locally and to England, was provided by a growing network of rolling roads and the development of Alexandria as a seaport. The final component, labor, for growing and transporting tobacco was provided in Fairfax County—just as it had been since 1660 in Virginia—by slaves. And it was the issue of slavery that was one of the key causes leading the country to civil war.

When the English established Jamestown, business investors in the Virginia Company of London were looking for profits by finding "precious metals or minerals, and valuable plants for dyestuffs and medicines, but they were prepared to settle for glass, iron, furs, potash, pitch, and tar, things that England needed and mostly had to import from other countries."[14]

Interestingly enough, the colonists failed to plant enough crops to provide for themselves and were dependent on shipments of food from England and the Indians to survive. The reasons are startling. A predominate factor was the large number of "gentlemen" who came to Jamestown. These gentlemen unfortunately had no manual skills, nor were they prepared to perform manual labor. The laborers who accompanied them were the personal attendants of the gentlemen, mainly footmen. The majority of the laborers in Jamestown never did any real work. Gentlemen, on the other hand, paid their way, something that supported the Virginia Company. In fact, gentlemen were too plentiful. Skilled laborers, who were to work as indentured servants for seven years to pay for their passage and then take advantage of their own opportunities, were too few.[15]

A Dutch sea captain brought the first twenty slaves to Virginia in 1619. However, the use of slaves didn't become profitable until 1660, due to the cost of a slave being twice that of an indentured servant. Also, the English had short lives in the new land. Only 50 percent of the colonists arriving in Virginia survived longer than five years. The cost of the purchase of a lifelong slave was both prohibitive and unnecessary. [16]

Work for the indentured servants in Virginia was harder than working in England. Servants had little incentive to work since they would eventually be free to pursue their own interests, and their masters had little reason to treat their servants well as they would be gone after their period of servitude. Not surprisingly, a master began to take increasingly strong measures to get his "full quota of work from his servants." By the 1620s, indentured servants were already beginning to be treated as possessions, necessary parts in the labor system, rather than human beings. Tobacco barons in Virginia began to buy, sell and beat their servants in their pursuit of riches. The result was positive, as by the 1640s the English tobacco barons could live more comfortably in Virginia than most men did in England.[17]

The tide turned to buying slaves in Virginia in 1660 for a number of reasons. The local duty paid on buying slaves was removed, reducing their cost from the Dutch sea captains. The supply of willing laborers from England was dwindling, while the life expectancy of the English living in Virginia was increasing, and "the slave became a better buy than the servant." But, due to low tobacco prices in England, only those growing tobacco in large quantities could count on making a profit, hence the need for more labor and more slaves.[18]

As with the indentured servants, slaves similarly had no incentive to work. By the time Virginians began to buy slaves, however, they were already practiced in the art of making them work. Lazy English servants were threatened by beatings and extensions of their period of servitude. Slaves were now made to fear for their lives through increasingly severe beatings, as freedom was no longer an option.

Tobacco would become profitable in the colonies due to slave labor. Virginia imported 45,000 slaves between 1700 and 1750. Tobacco was also the economic base of Fairfax County. By 1749, slaves predominated labor in the county.[19]

By the time of the American Revolution in 1776, to say Virginia had the prevailing influence in affairs leading to obtaining America's independence would be an understatement. Virginia was the largest territory and had the largest population in the new United States. Virginians owned the most slaves, over 40 percent of all slaves in the new nation. These slaves also grew the most tobacco in the country.[20]

Two men from Fairfax County had a direct effect on the American Revolution. George Washington, from Mount Vernon in southeast Fairfax County, was the leader of the Continental army and was the country's first president. George Mason, who lived at Gunston Hall, five miles south of Mount Vernon, wrote the first state constitution with a bill of rights. Virginians helped to write the Declaration of Independence, the United States Constitution and its first ten amendments. Their influence was also felt in other matters. They were all slaveholders.[21]

In the beginning of the nineteenth century, Fairfax County itself was changing. In 1801 Alexandria was removed from Fairfax County and became a part of Washington. The population of the county in 1810 was 13,111: 6,626 white and 7,028 black. Although it was not part of Fairfax County at the time, Alexandria had a total population of 7,227, with 4,093 white and 1,488 slaves, with the remaining few as free blacks, foreigners and Indians. These comparative sets of numbers indicate the difference between the rural area with more blacks than whites, signifying a higher ratio of slaves in the agricultural areas while in the city, close to a four to one ratio of whites to blacks.[22]

Fairfax County suffered a drop in population in the 1820s and 1830s, as people began migrating away after generations of tobacco farming had depleted the soil. The population of the county dropped 33 percent, to a total of 9,206—4,893 white and 4,313 black. Due to the poor condition of the soil, land began selling at a loss, and farmers began to work smaller plots of land, diversifying their crops, and eventually needed fertilizers to revitalize the soil.[23]

Immigrants from Europe who came to work on roads and bridges settled in the county. Some of the large landholders sold their property or divided it among their children, changing the pattern of land ownership from the plantation system to smaller and more prosperous farms. By 1840 the decline in county residents had ceased, and population rose to a total of 9,338 with slightly fewer blacks (42 percent) than whites (58 percent).[24]

These changes in the conditions and population in Fairfax County, as well as slavery in the early nineteenth century, can be traced through life at the Hope Park plantation, a few miles southwest of Fairfax Court House. Purchased in 1838 from the original owners from 1750, John Barnes and his family give us an idea of life in Fairfax County leading up to the Civil War.[25]

In the two decades before the Civil War, reformed farming methods led farmers to increased agricultural production and resultant increases in the population in Fairfax County as well as in the upper South. The population increase in both was due in part to the influx of Yankee Northerners with their industrious skill and effort in improving farm methods. The addition of Fairfax Station on the Orange and Alexandria Railroad, two miles from Hope Park, also brought new prosperity to southern Fairfax County by providing improved transportation to the market in Alexandria. The

Alexandria, Loudoun and Hampshire Railroad opened in 1860 from Alexandria to Farmwell (Ashburn), traveling through Falls Church, Vienna and Herndon, improved transportation to farmers in the northern end of the county.[26]

Slavery underwent a transformation in Fairfax County as well. Holding large numbers of slaves became unprofitable in a depressed economy in the middle nineteenth century. Nine to ten thousand slaves were actually being exported to the south and west from Virginia annually as they were too costly to keep. "Alexandria became headquarters for the largest slave-trading business in the entire south," as the Compromise of 1850 ended slave trading in Washington. This did not end the use of slaves in the city, but merely moved the slave trading business outside of the city limits.[27]

Owners of smaller plantations and large farms found it more beneficial for family members to use a mixture of labor, working alongside their slaves and hiring free outside laborers, than to use slaves as the principal workers. The outlay and cost of slaves was too high for the Barnes family, who had three strong sons to work the farm. Slave labor, however, remained a part of the labor force. In the 1840s, the Barnes family owned four slaves, seven in 1850, and by 1860 had grown to twelve as the Hope Park plantation grew in prosperity.[28]

Elsewhere in Fairfax County, there were twenty to thirty estates of comparable or greater value to the Hope Park plantation, and there were over two hundred county residents who owned an equal or greater number of slaves.[29]

By 1860 the population of Fairfax County had risen to 11,834. The white population totaled 68 percent and the percentage of slaves decreased to 27 percent, with the balance in free blacks at 5 percent. The population in Alexandria had risen to 12,652.[30] Life for the Barnes family, as well as many of the other families in Fairfax County, was indeed good, until the next few years when tumultuous events would cause catastrophic changes in their fortunes, lives and homeland.

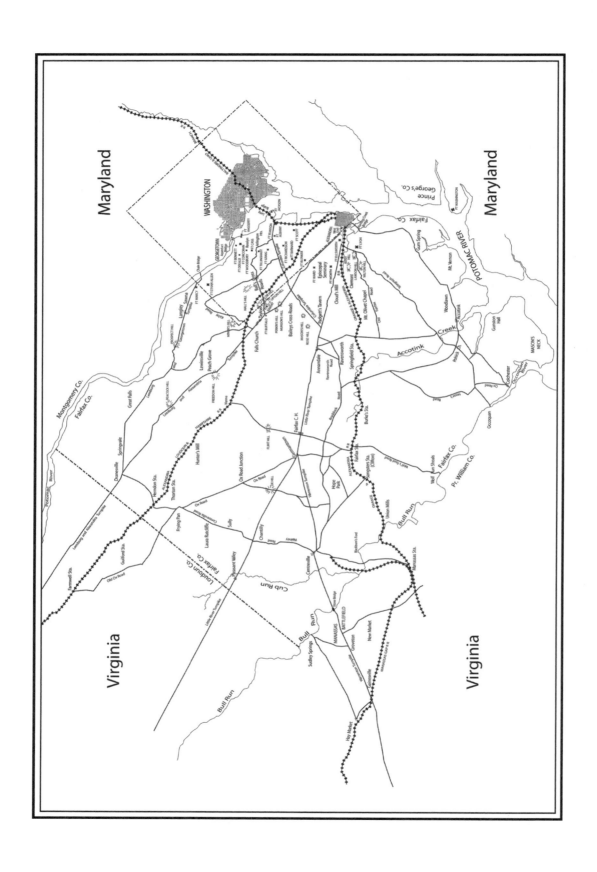

SECESSION

November 6, 1860, was Presidential Election Day, the day the residents of Fairfax County went to the polls. The results showed 685 men with Southern allegiances voting for John C. Breckinridge of the Southern Democratic Party, while a total of 807 voted for "Unionist" candidates, 692 for John C. Bell of the Constitutional Union Party, 91 for Stephen A. Douglas of the Northern Democrats and the lowest number of votes, 24, for Republican Abraham Lincoln.[31]

Voting was held in six districts in the county with two locations in each district and some polling places in private citizens' homes. Voting was held in western District No. 1 in Centreville and Sangster's Station. The southern District No. 2 included Littleton Hall and Charles A. Arundle's house. District No. 3 in the southeast portion of the county included Woodlawn Hills and the house of George M. Millan. The eastern District No. 4 included Annandale and Harriet O'Neale's house. District No. 5 included Fairfax Court House and Lewinsville crossroads in the center of the county. The northwestern District No. 6 included Dranesville and the house of John Ross.[32]

One immediate reaction and an indication of strong feelings of some residents in the county the day after the election was the chasing of a Lincoln supporter man out of town from the steps of the Fairfax Court House. A number of anti-Lincoln men blackened the man with printer's ink, put him on his horse and sent him home.[33]

A month later a crowd gathered at the Courthouse again, this time to debate Virginia's future after Lincoln's election. Representing the most radical faction of the community,

Facing page: The major locations and roads in Fairfax County during the Civil War based on the military map of northeastern Virginia and the vicinity of Washington compiled for General Irvin McDowell, August 1, 1862. *Steve Wolfsberger.*

one group resolved that Lincoln's election "constituted an act of aggression upon the rights of the states and was a direct attack on the institution of slavery." They "determined that the state had a right to secede and resist the passage of coercive forces through her territory." It was also "resolved that Virginians holding future Federal offices under the Lincoln administration would be deemed untrue to the state." The last sentiment of the pro-Southern gathering was that "the persons who had voted the Black republican ticket should be requested to remove to the free states where they can find sympathizers." The fear of slave insurrections sent slave patrols into the county in the areas of Langley, Frying Pan, Sangster's Station, Centreville and Fairfax Court House.[34]

The situation was somewhat calmer in Alexandria, although one businessman was confronted with the charge that he had been "monopolizing in Yankee trade," even selling the *New York Tribune*. Ardent Southerners "cautioned him to amend his ways if he knew what was good for him." In neighboring Washington, politicians, members of their families and the members of other wealthy families realized the rift between North and South was coming, and feelings based on their ancestral ties were beginning to surface. Thousands of Southerners would leave Washington in the spring of 1861 with the news of oncoming Secession. A flood of Northerners entered the city, taking the departed Southerners' places with the change of administration.[35]

A few months earlier, South Carolina had been the first state to secede from the Union in December 1860. Civilians were forming Home Guard units and putting their Southern sympathies into action for the protection of Alexandria and Fairfax County. The Mount Vernon Guards, the Alexandria Riflemen, the Alexandria Artillery and the Old Dominion Rifles formed in Alexandria, followed by the Fairfax Cavalry, organized by Mottram Dulany Ball, in Lewinsville. The Fairfax Rifles formed with recruits from Fairfax County in the spring of 1861.[36]

The citizens of Fairfax County had their own decision to make on the issue of Secession. In January 1861, Virginia Governor John Lechter authorized the election of delegates for a convention to determine the issue for the state. The race was on for a delegate from Fairfax County. William H. Dulaney ran on a Unionist platform and Alfred Moss ran on a Secessionist platform. Both men took the opportunity to state their views to a large gathering of civilians at Fairfax Court House on the monthly court date. The vote on February 4 was held in the six districts in the county, again with the majority of the citizens voting for the Unionist candidate. Dulaney received 57 percent of the vote to 43 percent for Moss in a heavy turnout of 1,464 voters. The vote, however, went the other way with 62 percent to 38 percent in favor to hold a statewide referendum to ratify the decision of Secession. The vote was held on the same day that seven states of the lower South met in Montgomery, Alabama, to form the Confederate States of America.[37]

The resulting convention in Richmond was indecisive until April 12, when Fort Sumter was fired on and President Lincoln subsequently called for 75,000 troops to put down the "insurrection." These actions moved the Virginia delegates' votes toward Secession, eighty-eight to fifty-five, on April 17. James W. Jackson, owner of the Marshall House hotel in Alexandria, raised the first Confederate flag in the city, proclaiming the prophetic words, "Whoever should attempt to remove it, would have to pass over his dead body."[38]

HOW VIRGINIA WAS VOTED OUT OF THE UNION.

Voter intimidation showing Secessionist fever in Fairfax County. *Fairfax County Public Library, Photographic Archives.*

Dulaney, true to his convictions, voted against Secession for Fairfax County, but the matter would be decided by an Ordinance of Secession to be put before a public vote by the citizens themselves on May 23. On April 27, the pro-Secessionist citizens of Fairfax County did not wait for the vote. At a public meeting at the courthouse they adopted twelve resolutions for the common defense of the county as well as forming a Committee of Safety and a Central Home Guard. "The committee was also given the authority to oversee the peaceable removal from the county of any person found to be disloyal to the Commonwealth."[39]

Of the 1,231 votes that were cast a week later on the issue of Secession, 76 percent were now in favor of the Ordinance of Secession, representing the Secession fever taken Fairfax County or the coercion that came with it. As the testimonials of a number of claimants before the Southern Claims Commission stated, anti-ordinance, pro-Union men were afraid to even go to the polls, were threatened to be killed if they actually showed up and four who first voted against seceding were subsequently "persuaded" to change their votes to go along with the Secessionist majority.[40]

Voting against the ordinance was indeed risky business. John W. Deavers described his peril as he voted. "When we went to Accotink to vote of the Ordinance of Secession, the Rebels had thrown old Mr. Plaskett out of the door. I came out and told them they could not throw me out of doors. Old Willie Henderson came to me at the election and told me if I did not vote for Secession I would be taken in the woods and hung. I told him if I was hung I would die for a good cause."[41]

With two locations added for the vote, only three of the fourteen locations tallied a majority of voters against the ordinance. The three were in Accotink in the Third District, perhaps representing the Quaker influence in the area, which included two members of the Gillingham family, and Lewinsville and Lydecker's in the Fifth District, indicating strong localized opinion against the ordinance. The following day, on May 24, 1861, Governor Lechter issued a proclamation that Virginia had seceded.[42]

Fairfax County would see only one major battle in the upcoming war. It would, however, be occupied continuously from the first day Union troops invaded the South to the last day as they returned to Washington for the Grand Review. The county lay on the doorstep of the city of Washington, the symbol of the North, the capital desired by the South that would be heavily defended by the orders of its president, Abraham Lincoln. Its civilians would suffer the depredations brought by both Union and Confederate armies daily throughout the ordeal. And those civilians whose homes and land stood in the way of the ravaging armies would have their homes, property and resources destroyed, their lives changed forever as the war unfolded.

THE ARMIES ARRIVE

In late April 1861, following the firing on Fort Sumter, President Lincoln initiated a blockade of Southern states including Virginia. Businesses in Alexandria suffered immediately. Flour was becoming scarce as Federal authorities confiscated it to feed the growing Union army in the capital. Prices increased as fewer supplies reached the port. Alexandria began to resemble a military camp, filled with troops with Southern ties drilling in the city, preparing for an advance of Federal troops from Washington.[43]

Schools in Fairfax, such as the Episcopal Seminary two miles west of Alexandria, closed as students headed North or South to return to their families. The civilians of Fairfax ceased to travel to Alexandria for fear the army would confiscate their carts and horses. "Frightened almost to death" of a Yankee attack, many civilians whose loyalties were with the South were leaving Alexandria. The Quaker Chalky Gillingham from Philadelphia, who had purchased two thousand acres from the Woodlawn Plantation and one thousand acres from the Mount Vernon estate, nine miles south of Alexandria, left his house and traveled to Maryland to stay with a friend, in fear of the "rebel soldiers coming and encamping all around us to attack the City of Washington."[44]

Civilians of both Northern and Southern sympathies did not have long to wait. Lincoln dared not "invade" Virginia soil until the Ordinance of Secession was passed on May 23. At 2:00 a.m. on the following morning, Federal regiments crossed the Long Bridge out of Washington and the Aqueduct Bridge out of Georgetown into Virginia, under the commands of Majors Charles W. Sanford, W.H. Wood, Samuel P. Heintzelman and Colonel Orlando B. Wilcox, while others under Colonel Elmer Ellsworth crossed the Potomac River by boat. Union troops converged on Southern soil for the first time to

A civilian's house taken for a Union army's headquarters for General Heintzelman at Fort Lyon just outside Alexandria in eastern Fairfax County, 1863. *Fairfax County Public Library, Photographic Archives.*

occupy Alexandria. On the same day they sent scouting parties into Falls Church and Ball's Cross Roads in Fairfax. The invasion of the South and the consequences thereof had begun with the invading forces beginning to erect fortifications at daybreak.[45]

Just ahead oncoming Union troops, all the Confederate troops stationed in Alexandria in what they realized was an indefensible city left on the Orange and Alexandria Railroad, crossing Fairfax County to mass with other Confederate troops in Manassas. The presence of Confederate troops in Fairfax had also begun.[46]

The first civilian casualty of the war occurred on May 24, the same day the Union troops entered Alexandria. Colonel Ellsworth marched directly to the Marshall House hotel to take down the Confederate flag flown there by the owner James W. Jackson. Coming down the stairs from the roof with the flag in his hands, Ellsworth was shot and killed by Jackson, who in turn was shot and killed by one of Ellsworth's men, Sergeant Francis E. Brownell. Jackson's vow to defend the Confederate flag fulfilled, the bloodshed of the war commenced.[47]

Anne Frobel, a staunchly loyal Southerner who lived in southeast Fairfax just outside Alexandria in her father's home "Wilton Hill," entered her first dated entry in a diary on May 24, a practice she would continue daily throughout the war. This diary provides us with her perspective as a civilian throughout the entire war. On this day she wrote, "I never saw 'Wilton' my dear old home looking more lovely and inviting. The trees and plants had put on their loveliest spring attire, and the garden was resplendent with the bloom of rare and brilliant flowers, and the fields were all smiling with a bright prospect of an abundant harvest. Every thing about the place was in order and shewed [sic] a high state of cultivation." Her idyllic view of the world and home would change that very day.[48]

On the next day, May 25, the consumption and destruction of private civilians' property in Alexandria would begin. The invading troops, looking for quarters, searched through the vacant homes of Secessionists, confiscating or destroying property as they went. Colonel Wilcox demanded stables and forage from the City Council for his First Michigan Cavalry. Failing to obtain compliance, Wilcox put Alexandria under martial law. His soldiers simply took whatever they wanted. When the *Alexandria Gazette* suspended publication rather than print the proclamation of martial law, Wilcox's troops simply seized the presses and printed it themselves.[49]

Regiment after regiment would move in and out of Alexandria during the war. The local residents named them the "Seven Year Locusts." In Fairfax, the same day Anne Frobel wrote her first entry in her diary, she tried to ride into Alexandria. Stopped by local men, she was warned "Linckton's [sic] men are there, got there only this morning, and there is no telling what they will do." She turned around and headed home, not realizing that Lincoln's men would soon arrive on her doorstep as well as in the rest of Fairfax.[50]

The beginning of the war signaled an end to the plantation life in Fairfax. The few schoolhouses located off of plantations were closed. John Barnes's three sons at Hope Park traveled the short distance to Fairfax Court House and joined the Seventeenth Regiment of Virginia Infantry, known as the Fairfax Rifles. With the men gone, the remaining family members and slaves were temporarily forced to abandon Hope Park only to return a short time later, lucky to find their house still standing but vandalized by Union soldiers. Chalky Gillingham would return to his house near Mount Vernon, believing the Southern troops had given up on their plans to attack Washington. He found his house intact, but had to search for his cattle. He was outside the protection of Union lines and constantly on guard against "rebel troops coming into the neighbourhood and carrying off men, horses, waggons and provisions."[51]

June of 1861 would signal the beginning of permanent change for the entire area around Washington. For the city's defense, fortifications were immediately constructed surrounding the city including those in Fairfax. Three forts, Corcoran, Haggerty and Bennett, guarded the Aqueduct Bridge from Georgetown. Forts Runyon and Albany guarded the Long Bridge to Washington. Fort Ellsworth was built just west of Alexandria. Fairfax County had quickly seen the armies and the forts come, and as James Barber writes, "The entire Virginia countryside seemed alive with white tents and raw red clay fortifications." These forts were built in fields and orchards, displacing dwelling and even churches without regard to their owners. And it was only the beginning.[52]

Major Irvin McDowell, in charge of organizing the Union forces in Virginia, immediately found himself with a lack of food for his men and fodder for his animals. He was directed to keep records for reimbursement of the local civilians for destruction of their property and occupation of their land. Records and reimbursements, however, were the last thing on the Union army's mind as it was attempting to organize itself while saddled with poor communications, tools and equipment. McDowell had to issue his own orders to his troops prohibiting the "trespass, depredations, and attempts at burglary" in Virginia.[53]

In May, Fairfax Court House was outside Union lines in eastern Fairfax County although patrols and skirmishing occurred daily. A company of the Confederate Warrenton Rifles had established camp at the courthouse as an outpost to protect the growing body of Confederates at Manassas just outside the western end of the county. On June 1, the cavalry of the Second U.S. Regulars rode past the courthouse, firing into the Confederates and killing their captain, John Quincy Marr, making him the first officer killed in the war.[54]

Following the Union dash through the courthouse, the Sixty-ninth New York Infantry arrested five Secessionists at Ball's Cross Roads on June 7. The Union army was expanding west through the county. Camp Mansfield was established at the crossing of the Alexandria, Loudoun and Hampshire Railroad and the Aqueduct Road, now Wilson Boulevard. Camp McDowell and Camp Upton were established on Upton's Hill just southeast of Falls Church, and Camp Tyler was established at Taylor's Tavern in Falls Church at the corner of present-day East Broad and Roosevelt Streets.[55]

On June 1, Anne Frobel reacted to the Union soldiers who had reached her house: "And now the war fare between us and this vile refuse of the earth begins in earnest. They came day—and night—any all daylong. The first thing in the morning, before I am up I hear their vile abusive, scurrilous, blasphemy, O how can we live through it to have our peaceful home thus invaded." She also wrote in her diary how the "demons" came into her kitchen and just took whatever food they could get their hands on. She also recorded her impressions of the New York Zouaves, "O the horrible, horrible red legs, the fire Zouaves, here they come again with the tight blue skull caps and long cords and tassels hanging from the top knot. I think if possible they are more savage than the rest."[56]

Confederate activity was increasing in Fairfax County, and Union forces were sent to scout such activity on June 17. Union troops under Brigadier General Robert C. Schneck were sent to Vienna on the Alexandria, Loudoun and Hampshire Railroad. The train was ambushed within a quarter-mile of the village of Vienna by Confederate soldiers of the First South Carolina Infantry, who upon hearing the train whistle, quickly deployed their men and fired two guns at the oncoming train, killing eight Union soldiers in a Confederate victory.[57]

Troops from both sides continued to scout and probe the central area of Fairfax County. In late June, a war correspondent from the *New Orleans Daily True Delta* described the area at Fairfax Station as he wrote, "The whole country around seems a continuous camp. Fortifications bristle up in every direction. All Virginia is now on a formidable footing of war." The correspondent's prophecy that Virginia was "now on a formidable footing of war" was soon to be realized, as within a few short weeks 35,000 Union soldiers would march west from Alexandria and Washington across the twenty-eight-mile-wide county to the first battle of the war in Manassas.[58]

Falls Church was the most forward or western front in the county, just over four miles southwest of Washington, with twelve thousand Union soldiers under General Tyler camping there. On July 16, they started their march to Manassas through Fairfax Court House, first by marching west on the Leesburg Turnpike, then east on Columbia Turnpike at Bailey's Cross Roads to Annandale and then on to Fairfax Court House on the Little River Turnpike. Union troops moved across the Potomac to Alexandria and Arlington Heights and to Bush Hill, five miles into Fairfax County, under the command of Colonel O.O. Howard, also moving toward Manassas on the sixteenth.[59]

Annandale saw the influx of thousands of Union soldiers on July 16, including the Union army's leader, General McDowell. Colonel Ambrose Burnside led his men from Rhode Island and New York into the village along the Columbia Turnpike, General Hunter led five thousand men of the Second Division and Colonel Dixon Miles led five thousand of his men in the Fifth Division. Skirting the congestion in Annandale, General Samuel Heintzelman's Third Division was marching west from Alexandria on Franconia Road, as was General Daniel Tyler's First Division on the Chain Bridge Road.[60]

After spilling into every empty space available, thousands of campfires burned in and around Annandale, only to be extinguished the following morning of June 17 as the troops marched west on Ravensworth Road, Braddock Road and the Little River Turnpike through Fairfax Court House and then onto the Warrenton Turnpike, today's Lee Highway, to Centreville. Elements of the Union army passed through Vienna, across Pohick Creek and past Sangster's Station and Wolf Run Shoals on their way to Centreville.[61]

From July 18 to July 21, the first major battle was fought, first at Blackburn's Ford, south of Centreville along Bull Run, straddling Fairfax and Prince William Counties, and then at Manassas in Prince William County. After the Confederate victory and Union defeat, the Union soldiers fled east back across Fairfax County, along the Warrenton Turnpike through Centreville, and on through Fairfax Court House, Annandale and Falls Church into the forts and camps they had just left a few days earlier as well as back into Alexandria and Washington.

Anne Frobel could not refrain in her exultation: "I suppose it is not right to exult over a fallen foe. But there certainly was one wide spread note of rejoicing throughout the whole section of the country when we learned that the whole regiment of N.Y. City fire Zouaves were completely exterminated, and I sent up my heart-felt thanks with the rest."[62]

Although victorious, the Confederate army was in no shape to take the offensive. The army was badly disorganized and also severely lacking in supplies. Within hours of their victory, Confederate troops crossed Bull Run, rummaging for food in the abandoned Union campsites near Centreville. Within a week, Confederates had advanced east from Manassas to Fairfax Court House "as much to gather supplies left by the Federals as to shove Confederate lines toward the Northern Capital."[63]

By July 23, Confederates were moving into Falls Church and subsequently driving Union infantry farther east. General James Longstreet moved his Confederate Advanced Forces headquarters to Falls Church in August and September and was joined by General J.E.B. Stuart. One day after First Manassas, Major General Gustavus Woodson Smith and Generals Joseph E. Johnston and P.G.T. Beauregard met and received instructions from Confederate President Jefferson Davis at Fairfax Court House.[64]

J.E.B. Stuart's regiment, including Private John Singleton Mosby, camped at Fairfax Court House with other Confederate forces on July 23. Union troops retreated farther out of Fairfax County as Confederate forces took over Bailey's Cross Roads, Ball's Cross Roads, Munson's Hill and Mason's Hill, just outside the Union ring of forts in the most eastern portion of the county. Longstreet's forces were even stationed on the heights outside Annandale, just three miles from Alexandria and six from Washington, to provide warnings of enemy movement. The majority of Fairfax County was back in Confederate hands. From their high vantage points on the occupied hills, they could count windowpanes in Washington, view the Capitol dome and identify church spires in Georgetown.[65]

In the aftermath of First Manassas, President Lincoln appointed General George B. McClellan of the Union forces in Washington on July 27. In August, McClellan ordered Major John G. Barnard to construct forty-eight forts around Washington, the majority of which would be constructed by the end of 1861. By 1865, a total of sixty-two named forts would be built in a circle around Washington for its defense. Over half (thirty-three) would be located in Fairfax County. Additional earthworks in Fairfax included twenty-five batteries, seven blockhouses and fieldworks every eight hundred to one thousand yards covering all the important approaches to Washington. Rifle pits and military roads connected the majority of the forts, whose armament included 265

Confederate General P.G.T. Beauregard's headquarters at Fairfax Court House. The house, belonging to William T. Rumsay, would also serve as the headquarters of Union General George B. McClellan after the Confederates pulled out of Fairfax in the spring of 1862. *Fairfax County Public Library, Photographic Archives.*

smoothbore cannons, 170 rifled cannons and 60 mortars. The easternmost portion of the county surrounding Washington would subsequently be heavily defended and duly manned by tens of thousands of Union soldiers throughout the war.[66]

After First Manassas, Confederate forces continued to occupy Fairfax into the fall including the areas of Fairfax Court House, Centreville, Accotink, Lewinsville, Falls Church, Frying Pan, Munson's Hill, Mason's Hill, Taylor's Hill, Bailey's Cross Roads and Ball's Cross Roads. These troops were the front lines protecting the mass of Confederate troops in Manassas warning of any Union offensive from the most eastern portion of the county, Washington, and Alexandria.

Union troops did not, however, sit idle. The close proximity of the opposing armies led to frequent skirmishes. On July 29, the Thirty-seventh New York Infantry skirmished with Confederates near Falls Church. On August 8, Union Captain William H. Boyd, First New York, Lincoln Cavalry, charged twenty Confederate cavalry near Pohick Church.[67]

Lewinsville, described as "a little hamlet consisting of a church and three to four houses," saw three battles in the month of September alone. The first Battle of Lewinsville occurred when General J.E.B. Stuart's Confederate forces routed Union troops on the evening of September 10. The Union soldiers again marched on Lewinsville on the fourteenth as a show of force only to be routed again by the Confederates. On the twenty-fifth, the Confederates again easily bested a larger number of Union soldiers for the third time.[68]

Curiously, the presidents of both countries visited Fairfax County in the same month. In September, Confederate President Jefferson Davis visited General Beauregard at his headquarters at Fairfax Court House. General J.J. Johnston was also present, and Beauregard presented a plan to Davis requesting reinforcements to move in Pennsylvania and Maryland as the path to capturing Washington. The plan was not approved as a defensive posture and was adopted to protect the borders of Virginia. United States President Abraham Lincoln rode in his carriage to Fort Marcy on September 8 to ensure that his stay of execution was received for Private William Scott, Company K, Third Regiment of the Vermont Volunteers, who was charged with falling asleep on his post while on picket duty. On September 10, Lincoln again ventured into Fairfax, this time to Fort Ethan Allen, one half-mile from Fort Marcy, to review the soldiers with General McClellan.[69]

Reconnaissance movements, skirmishes, ambushes, raids and the building of entrenchments and fortifications would continue into the fall by both sides of the conflict. In October, however, a major change would occur in the Confederate plans and positions. General Joseph Johnston gave orders on October 19 to pull all Confederate forward positions back to Centreville. This included the troops at Munson's Hill, Mason's Hill, Falls Church and Fairfax Court House. The decision was made based on the inability of the Confederate forces to go on the offensive, so Johnston decided to consolidate his forces to reduce the danger of the troops on the front lines.[70]

Skirmishing continued as Union troops immediately moved forward into the areas vacated by the Confederates into Fairfax County. On November 20, with little possibility of major action during the oncoming winter, General McClellan and President Lincoln held a Grand Review of up to one hundred thousand Union troops in the fields between Munson's Hill and Bailey's Cross Roads.[71]

A month later, the last action of the year would take place on December 20, as Colonel J.E.B. Stuart went on a foraging expedition from Centreville to Dranesville with 150 men. Union Brigadier General Edward Ord came upon Stuart's scattered troops and was able to force Stuart to retire back to Centreville. Following the Battle of Dranesville, General Johnston put his 40,000 troops into winter quarters in Centreville.[72]

What, however, happened to the citizens in Fairfax County in this first year of the war? Their stories are many.

Robert and Ann Coleman lived through the Battle of Dranesville. They lived in the east end of Dranesville at the termination of the Alexandria and Georgetown Turnpike, where they owned a country store with dry goods and groceries. Dranesville "was a little village, [only] fifteen or twenty houses." During the battle, the Colemans and their son hid in their cellar. The house was hit by eleven cannonballs and two exploded. The house and furniture were nearly destroyed. They left the day after the battle and returned home after the war. When they returned, the house was totally gone. "No, not a particle of it. Not a piece if it. The Coleman's were told that Major Taggert took it for quarters. Took the house all to pieces and built huts of it. The Union soldiers were in camp in Dranesville all that winter."[73]

A unique insight provided by a "loyal Northerner" belongs to the aunt of Confederate General Robert E. Lee, who owned the largest property in Fairfax County for which a claim was made to the Southern Claims Commission after the war. Mrs. Anna Maria Fitzhugh lived on the 8,007-acre Ravensworth estate in Annandale during the war in order to protect the house.[74]

Her husband's niece, Mary Anna Randolph Custis, was married to the most famous of Confederate generals. Anna Maria knew Robert E. Lee from his boyhood and considered him "one of the kindest friends I ever had." Just prior to the war, she said his "mind was distressingly exercised" on "the anxiety of the Virginia people [and] that he should be amongst them, that he should take command of their army."

She came to the realization that he had decided to join the Southern cause on the morning he decided to go to Richmond. He had sent her a farewell message stating that he had gone to Richmond and that it was too early in the morning to visit her. He had been in Alexandria the day before, and they had gone to church together. She recalled she was putting on her bonnet when he arrived, and that he stepped out of the carriage and sent word that he was there to go to church with her. They talked on the way to church that Sunday and he told her "that he had made up his mind what he wanted to do. He drew a distinction between Virginia and the general matter of Secession. I always thought that was the reason that influenced him, that he didn't like to turn his back, or his hand upon his own state, and his own children. He was very much disturbed and concerned."

Mrs. Fitzhugh's recollection as recounted was accurate. The Sunday she attended Christ Church in Alexandria with Lee was April 21, 1861. Lee had been offered

Union troops in control of Bailey's Cross Roads, circa 1862. *Fairfax County Public Library, Photographic Archives.*

command of the Union armies on Thursday, April 18 and resigned his commission from the U.S. Army on Saturday, April 20. Lee left Alexandria by train for Richmond early on Monday morning, April 22. He received command of the military forces of Virginia in Richmond the following day on Tuesday, April 23.[75]

As to the First Battle of Manassas, she recalled that "there were numbers and numbers [of Union soldiers] quartered" at Ravensworth before the battle. She had a Federal guard at her door. She had forgotten his name, but he told her "I am staying here to keep the soldiers from going into your kitchen." She recalled there were Confederate officers stationed within a half-mile of her house after the battle.

Ravensworth is a prime example of how civilian property was appropriated, as it provided an easy bonanza of timber for the Union army during the war. General Elias M. Greene, quartermaster of the Department of Washington, actually provided testimony in Mrs. Fitzhugh's claim to the Southern Claims Commission after the war that he was "quite familiar with Ravensworth estate, and he cut down over four thousand acres in wood." The wood was cut and taken during all four years of the war, starting in the winter of 1861. He wrote, "I found that wood could be cut and hauled from her estate at much less cost to the government than from other estates. First: Because of the saving of hauling to the [Springfield Station on the Orange and Alexandria] railway and secondly, because of the saving of guards [the cutting parties were under constant attack by Mosby's men], by putting a large party of cutters and teams into the woods at one place."

The commission did not believe Mrs. Fitzhugh's claim of loyalty to the North, however, especially in light of her lifelong association with the South's greatest general. In mid-May, his wife Mary Lee had moved to Ravensworth after Union forces occupied her house in Arlington. A colored driver, Henry Jackson from Alexandria, testified to the commission that he drove his hack to and from Ravensworth a couple of times in the early part of the war. He drove both Mrs. Fitzhugh and Mrs. Robert E. Lee. He heard both ladies "talk about the war saying that the Yankees had no business there. I know she was on Beauregard's side. I know it from what I heard her say."[76]

Interestingly enough, Jackson described his own conversations on the subject of his loyalty while driving his hack. "Sometimes when I got a drink or two ahead, I would talk as much as they did. Sometimes I was on the other side. I was on the side I got the money from. That's just what I did. I was not against the Yankees in my heart but when I was in Rome I would do as Rome done, but of course I wanted to be free. Sometimes a person has to talk a heap of ways."

James S. Purdy, who lived in Annandale, voted against the Ordinance of Secession, and faced the wrath of Confederates in the area for doing so. "When I voted against the Ordinance of Secession and advised others to do likewise, I drew down on myself the vengeance of the Confederate authority and nearly all my personal property they could lay their hands on was seized by order. I have now realized the fact, known in the south but not in the North, that the great sufferers by the war were the Unionists, who were stripped by both parties." Purdy claimed that after First Manassas on July 22, four or five Union soldiers stole four horses, two or more sets of harnesses and a large spring wagon to take the wounded to town. He would lose the rest of the buildings on his property during the rest of the war.[77]

Ambrose Cock Jr. lived on a 37¾-acre farm near Annandale. He claimed Brigadier General Louis Blenker's mostly German Forty-fifth New York Infantry took fodder (or corn) and fences in November 1861. This corresponds to the period after First Manassas when the Confederates pulled back to Centreville and the Union forces moved into Annandale. Blenker had a picket line that ran along an embankment that ran from Cock's farmhouse to the Little River Turnpike. He also claimed, "Mosby arrested me once for carrying news, [but] didn't keep me long."[78]

Maria Howard, who lived in Annandale, had a closer brush with Mosby. The California Battalion, attached to the Second Massachusetts Cavalry, fought Mosby right in front of her house, with Union soldiers taking refuge inside. Sergeant Short of the California Battalion said, "Mrs. Howard opened her house for them, and that he stood in the door, and fired several shots at Mosby and that he wounded Mosby." Sergeant Short and his men were escorting horses to the Union army when Mosby's men attacked them.[79]

Fort Lyon was located southwest of Alexandria along Telegraph Road and was the second largest—nine acres—of the forts surrounding Washington. Construction started in September 1861. It was built to control the heights south of Hunting Creek to protect Alexandria, a vital supply point for Washington, from being shelled. What material and supplies the soldiers did not receive from the quartermaster they simply took from the civilians in the surrounding neighborhood.[80]

Court H. Johnson claimed soldiers of the Sixteenth New York took his fence for floors in their tents at Fort Lyon even though "when the Union army came on I gave them straw for bedding. I gave them all I had. I did not like to see them lay on the bare ground."[81]

Fort Lyon was built on part of Thomas Pulman's farm. The Union troops pulled down his house. "Troops staid in our neighborhood all through the war. This house was on the place when I bought it. They built Fort Lyon in the cornfield. They used some of the biggest logs for the Fort." He was once arrested because his son sold whiskey to a soldier at the fort.[82]

John A. Fairfax had three acres of sod taken from his property for the slopes of Fort Lyon. Fairfax also had a distillery on his property. Union troops took 280 gallons of whiskey along with corn and oats. Lieutenant Colonel Farnum ordered Fairfax to distill two remaining mashes in mash tubs, put it in barrels and take it away for safekeeping. "I had to buy the coal and hire the men to run the engine to distill it." This was too much for the Union soldiers to stay away from. They eventually found the whiskey hidden in his barn and took it.

Colonel Ellsworth's New York Zouaves later destroyed the distillery after they had encamped on Shuter's Hill to the north where Fort Ellsworth was located. "When Ellsworth's Zouaves came down, we were running the distillery and separating the whiskey from the grain, and there was a portion of the mash that was not distilled,

Fort Lyon along Telegraph Road just southwest of Alexandria, circa 1862. *Fairfax County Public Library, Photographic Archives.*

and they stopped us and would not allow us to distill, and that was dumped out into the slop and fed to the hogs, and that made them drunk. They would stagger and squeal and fight like madmen." Mr. Fairfax's property was not only carried off. The U.S. government pastured four of five thousand head of cattle on his property where "they would eat everything off like grasshoppers."[83]

Residents in the West End, located between Fort Ellsworth and Alexandria, had their share of complaints when the fort was built. James Coleman was allowed money from the claims commission for fruit trees, a greenhouse that was taken to build quarters and pave streets and for ovens to bake bread for the soldiers at Fort Ellsworth. Colonel Franklin sent guards from his brigade to protect Coleman and his house. "I might as well have none for they would take things anyhow. There was no use to ask for receipts because the soldiers took it in peice meals, and my patience was worn out in fact."

Construction was started on Fort Ellsworth on May 25, 1861, just as the Union soldiers invaded Virginia. The soldiers cut down peach, apple, pear, cherry and damson plum trees to clear the way for a clear view from the fort. The soldiers who came for potatoes from August to September 1861 would "come with sacks, bags and

baskets and dig them out." The greenhouse that was taken was made of at least fifty thousand bricks. Most of the property was taken at night.[84]

On the same date, Anne Frobel attested to the quickly growing number of Union soldiers in Fairfax County and her fear of them: "From the porch here we can see now the groups of white tents dotted about the common and growing up each side of the [Alexandria, Loudoun and Hampshire] railroad, as yet we remain unmolested although we hear of parties of the military prowling all over the country committing all manner of depredations and violence."[85]

Fairfax Station and Burke Station were located on the Orange and Alexandria Railroad south of Fairfax Court House and were outside Union lines in 1861. Mary A. Gossom lived near Fairfax Station. She had little education and could neither read nor write. In her appeal to the Southern Claims Commission, she first dealt with Confederate soldiers. "The Rebel soldiers often abused me and threatened to shoot me because I wouldn't do anything for them. They never did me any harm except to take my fowls and now and then a hog. I have fed the soldiers and taken care of the sick and wounded. They were almost always camped around us. I lived on the Fredericksburg road. I have sat up with their sick many a time. I have got a few passes from the Rebels to go to and from the Court House. They never made me take any oath."

Union forage column at Camp Griffin in Langley, Virginia, circa 1862. Wagons such as these were used to collect needed food, fuel and supplies from civilians in the surrounding area. *Fairfax County Public Library, Photographic Archives.*

She then dealt with Union soldiers the day before First Manassas. "The soldiers came to my house about noon. They went to the stable and took the horse. I begged hard for him but they said an officer wanted him as his own had given out. My horse was a young one. I had bought him about a year [before] and gave $122.50 for him in Gold. The troops were marching by all that day and night. About evening they killed 11 hogs, skinned them and carried them off."[86]

Robert T. Scisson lived between Fairfax Court House and Fairfax Station to the south. He claimed Union troops took 120 bushels of oats and 9 hogs the day before First Manassas on their way to that battle. In his claim, one of the witnesses on his behalf stated,

> *Robert T. Sisson is an old Virginian who is strong and faithful to his country in every sense of the word. During the war he was surrounded by southerners and told he had to vote the "sesesh" ticket. He said "no gentlemen, not as long as the Sun rose and shone on [my] head would he vote to brake up the union." And he did not. He has stood and*

been beaten like an anvil ever since. And today he can look up from his poverty stricken home and thank God that the flag still waves over an undivided union.[87]

Robert Scission was not recorded as voting either for or against the Ordinance of Secession. His son Matthew, testifying on his father's behalf, said, "I was in favor of the Union. I took no part either way." So much for his honesty—and perhaps that of his father—as Matthew voted for the Ordinance of Secession at Fairfax Court House.[88]

Daniel Collins also lived near Fairfax Station with his wife Rebecca and made a claim for horses, corn and oats taken by Union troops on their way to First Manassas. Falling on hard times, Rebecca made the petition to the claims commission since her husband moved to Colorado in 1871 to support her struggling family. After 1873 she had not heard from him again. "I now rent a house near the station and take in sewing to support myself and family. My two oldest children are hired out and help me take care of the younger children. I have 7 children in all. I don't know whether he [my husband] is dead or alive, but I believe he is dead, for I don't think he would stop writing if he was living." The commission allowed $310 for the claim and recommended that the award be given to her.[89]

Civilians at Fairfax Court House suffered during the first year of the war. Charles Kirby owned a six-hundred-acre farm two miles north of Fairfax Court House. He provided a very detailed claim for damages after the war. In October 1861, he claimed six hundred bushels of oats, ten tons of hay and three hundred bushels of potatoes were taken by the men of Union General Smith. In November and December, he claimed one hundred cords of wood, two hundred bushels of corn and two hundred bushels of potatoes were taken by General Morrill's brigade. This was just as the Union army moved into the area of Fairfax Court House late in the year, after the Confederate troops pulled back to Centreville.[90]

Kirby was listed as voting against the Ordinance of Secession, yet his claim was rejected as he had not completely established his loyalty, although the commission did not find that he was actually disloyal. The problem lay in his conduct during the war. His neighbors disputed and denied his loyalty. He had three sons in the Confederate army and one son in the Union service. After First Manassas when the Confederates took control of most of the county, he left his house for six months and lived within Confederate lines in Chantilly, fifteen minutes from his house. This was considered a "strong presumptive of Confederate Sympathies, while all good Union men went in the opposite direction to Washington."[91]

In a reference to General McClellan's Grand Review in November 1861, Esther J. Ferguson of Fairfax Court House had her farm and household effects taken by the Rebels. "Our property was advertised to be sold the following Saturday, but on Wednesday General McClellan had a grand review at Bailey's Cross Roads and the rebels fell back from here and the sale was not made."[92]

William Purcell, who lived about one mile west of Bailey's Cross Roads, had his house used as a headquarters from September 1861 until January 1864. By the end of the war, he had lost his four-room house, smokehouse, stable, granary, sheds and corn house. He had ten acres of woodland, half of which was burned off for a parade ground and the other half cut for fuel.[93]

Glascoe Gaskins, a colored man who was born free and lived at Fairfax Station, did receive compensation after the war for two horses taken from him in July before First Manassas. He tried to follow his horses to the Union camp near Fairfax Station but was afraid to follow them into the camp: "I was always on the Union side, I did not know what the war was about but they told me it would be best for the colored people if the union men whipped [the Confederates] and I believed it."[94]

In Centreville, claims were made just before the battle of First Manassas. Mary E. Burke claimed Union "General [O.O.] Howard's Division camped on my place from Friday to Monday, the day of the 1st Bull Run Battle." (The day of the Battle of First Manassas, July 21, was actually on a Sunday.) She claimed the Union soldiers took corn, potatoes, yearlings, poultry, one horse and oats.[95]

Ann Murtaugh, who lived two miles from Centreville, presented a claim in the name of her deceased husband, Andrew. She claimed Rebels took her whole crop of corn—twenty acres—in the fall of 1861. "I was once told by a Confederate soldier that I would be taken away from home and my blood would have to answer for my Union sentiments. I had talked pretty saucy to him. He wanted me to bake some bread and I told him I could not. He charged me with being a Union woman, and I told him it was none of his business."[96]

The majority of claims in 1861 were made from civilians in the northeast quadrant of Fairfax County. These included claims from Vienna, Chain Bridge, Falls Church, Langley, Lewinsville, Upton's Hill, Bailey's Cross Roads and Prospect Hill. These were the areas largely controlled by Union forces where fortifications were built in the first months of the war.

In addition to the soldiers taking whatever resources they wanted from Anne Frobel, she suffered the "military necessity" of having Union officers live in her house. At the end of September, Ms. Frobel was informed that General Sedgwick's brigade was to occupy her property and that he was going to use her house as his headquarters. The Union officers suggested that Anne and her sister move into town and that wagons would be provided to move their belongings. Her sister Lizzie replied that they had no means to rent a house, so they had no choice but to stay. The two sisters were told "as to any losses we might sustain by the army the government would amply remunerate us for everything of that sort." Not only were the two sisters "forlorn and heart-stricken" they were concerned about the slaves that still lived and worked at Wilton Hill. "Wherever the yankees go they are sure to leave the free-negro mark behind them."[97]

Instead of General Sedgwick taking over their house, one of his married staff officers was selected to move in with his wife. Lieutenant Beaumont and his wife moved into the house with Anne and Lizzie Frobel for four to five months. Surprisingly, Anne found Mrs. Beaumont to be "a perfect lady, cultivated and refined. We never had the slightest fault with them: they treated us like older sisters so very kind and considerate and so afraid of saying or doing anything that might offend or wound our feelings."

However, Anne never trusted them, for she had a brother, Bushrod, in the Confederate army. "They were strangers to us and we were so afraid of them, we feared treachery in every word and act."[98]

Windows and doors seemed to be in demand by the Union army at Bailey's Cross Roads. Ambrose Barcroft of Barcroft Hill left his property after First Manassas in fear of Rebel soldiers who were within sight of his house. He returned in the fall of 1861 only to find Federal officers were occupying his house and Brigadier General Louis Blenker's division was camped on the property. Leaving again and returning in 1863, he found forty acres of timber on his ninety-acre farm had been cleared. "The troops took cows, hogs, wagon, and all the furniture left. Two houses were burned by the soldiers. Windows were taken from [the] houses and mill."

In a supporting deposition, a witness said, "The windows and doors were taken to Bailey's Cross Roads and used in a large building the Federals had put up." Mr. Barcroft's son was more specific about the windows and doors. "I saw a number of the doors and windows at Bailey's Cross Roads. I had recognized them from their peculiar make. I had them made in Philadelphia. There were 45 windows in all, 20 doors, and 6 barn doors."[99]

John Hall of Bailey's Cross Roads also had problems with the men of Blenker's Camp taking corn from his farm between September and October 1861. All of his buildings were destroyed. A neighbor provided a deposition on the destruction adding a tellingly simple observation, "He had a elegant, delightful fence."[100]

The burning of citizens' houses was a common theme in the claims. Nancy and Elcom Read had two frame houses burned at Bailey's Cross Roads. One witness testified that a Union captain ordered the buildings to be burned to prevent them from being used as cover for Rebel sharpshooters. Another witness, however, testified, "They were burned by Union troops about two weeks after the first battle of Bull Run. I was standing near when they set fire to those buildings. The men belonged to the second Michigan Vols. and were doing picket duty at the time. The rebel pickets were within a mile at the time. I asked the soldiers why they did so and burn them buildings. They told me were just making up a fire to roast some potatoes. I think they burned these buildings out of mischief."[101]

Letitia Strother of Vienna had what was probably a common family problem during the war. Her husband fought in the Confederate army under Mosby while her son fought for the Union. "[My son] left and went away with [Union] soldiers that stood around picketing. They were picketing around [the] house and he was down with them and they took him off with them. I didn't know he was going myself."[102]

Conscription into the Confederate army was a concern for residents of Vienna. Henry Biggs, who lived at Peacock Hill, four miles from Vienna, escaped conscription in the Confederate army by leaving his home and fleeing to Washington. He remained there during the war.[103]

Josiah B. Bowman of Vienna escaped conscription as well. "I tried to stay right here and keep as quiet as possible" until the Confederates pulled back to Manassas before First Manassas. "I heard we were to be conscripted or put into the militia and I came to Washington and stayed until the [Confederate] army went back. Union General Tyler made his headquarters in my house the first night after they left the defences of Washington to advance to Bull Run. I went back there again and he had gotten the house before I got there."[104]

General Tyler asked him to be a guide for him. Bowman didn't want his Southern neighbors to know he was going to act as a guide for the Union army, so he told his neighbors that one of his colored men went off with the Massachusetts troops. He claimed that his man didn't have his free papers and was put in jail, so Bowman was leaving to get him back. Bowman wasn't through telling fanciful stories.

After First Manassas, the Confederates took possession of Vienna and they "picketed us in…I had to remain home then. They [the Confederates] gave me no pass and I remained very quiet." On August 2, 1861, Confederate Colonels Bacon and Williams called him out of his home and demanded to know if he was Bowman. "I said I was, and they took me to the Provost Marshall, and [then] back to the [Alexandria, Loudoun and Hampshire] railroad in front of my house and put me in the woodshed under a guard. I staid there until the next afternoon. They took me to Centreville, then to Manassas under guard. The next morning I was sent to Richmond on the 8 o'clock train." Bowman was kept in Richmond until the twenty-second when he received a hearing, but refused to take the oath of allegiance to the Confederacy. "I told them I was better off where I was [in prison]."

That's when Mr. Bowman's storytelling served him again. At a later prisoner exchange, he was sent back to Washington by impersonating a German soldier also being held in Richmond. "They watched me pretty close [on the trip back to Washington], but they didn't detect me."

A more improbable story was the case presented before the Southern Claims Commission by Albert Orcutt, who joined Captain Mottram Ball's Confederate Fairfax Cavalry, voted for the Ordinance of Secession, then switched sides and became a scout and guide for the Union army. He actually proved his loyalty to the commission and received an allowance for damages he suffered by Union troops.

Orcutt claims to have voted for William H. Dulaney, the Unionist delegate for the convention to determine whether Virginia would secede or not. However, on May 24, 1861, the day after he voted for the Ordinance of Secession, Orcutt rode to Alexandria to join his Confederate company. Upon his arrival in Alexandria he was told that his unit had already been captured. He then rode to Fairfax Court House and then on to Manassas. He was then detailed to Fairfax Station, and from there back to Fairfax Court House. He asked for a fresh horse but was cursed at by a Captain Delany for riding his horse too fast and was refused a fresh mount. He was then requested to guide an officer and his cavalry to Vienna. After being provided a fresh horse, Orcutt took the cavalry to Vienna and helped post them as pickets. The next day, replacement pickets from the courthouse brought him his own horse and exchanged him for the borrowed horse.

It was at that point that he had had enough of being a Confederate soldier, and he decided to switch his allegiance. He hid in the woods near his place until dark. He then rode to the Union pickets stationed near Chain Bridge. "They halted me when

I was riding up and asked 'who goes there?' I says 'a Virginia soldier in full uniform.' They said 'What do you want here?' Says I, 'I want to go to Washington. I have an uncle there and I want to go there and put myself under his protection' and one of the officers in command says 'who is he?' I said 'he is Uncle Sam' and he ordered me to dismount and then he put me in the guard house until morning, and then brought me to General Mansfield, and I was released and had the privilege to go back to my home in Western N.Y."

Orcutt stayed in New York for three weeks, and then came back and was a guide for the Union army for a year and a half. During the war he had 125 panels of fencing taken by men of General Porter's division for stables for army horses as well as flooring for officer's tents and received an allowance for them. Orcutt had a number of witnesses provide depositions that he was truly a Union man. They explained he had only joined the Confederate cavalry at first to protect his property because he didn't think the war would go on for any great length of time. Once he saw the war would not be over as quickly as he thought, he changed his allegiance and supported his true sympathies.[105]

Lott W. Crocker lived on a dairy farm in Lewinsville. He did not vote for or against the Ordinance of Secession, as he had just moved to Virginia in 1860 and had no right to vote. He did, however, go to the poll in Lewinsville. "I went with my father to the polls, armed and equipped to protect him in his right to vote." Obviously, this would have been a vote against ratification of the Ordinance of Secession. Lott's brother, Francis, was recorded as voting against the Ordinance and was enlisted in the Union army. Lott's father likely was the J.D. Crocker listed as voting against the Ordinance as well.[106] Lott stated:

I used to bring in the mail from Langley to General Mansfield [at Camp Marcy] *and he requested me to stay there as long as I could. A portion of the time the rebels would not let me bring in milk; said they were going to starve out the city, and tried to make me go to Alexandria, but I would not do that, and carried it home. This was in the spring of 1861. I remained at home until the rebels captured my father, who was living with me. They took him to Culpeper and he died there. General* [W.F. "Baldy"] *Smith told me my place was between two camps. I had better not go home, but take my family away, which I did. I was acting as a guide for the army and was with Gen. Smith most every night. I did not probably go near my place twice in those two years.*

Benjamin D. Carpenter lived about three-quarters of a mile from Lewinsville and felt the local hostility toward Northerners. In the spring of 1861, he accepted a job in Washington with the government police. After First Manassas, his daughter said he had to leave his home because "as a Union man, his life was in danger. There was a reward out for his capture and he did not dare come home to sleep, but laid out with firearms to protect himself. Those who wanted to capture him were his closest neighbors."[107]

John Gilbert owned 160 acres of land near Lewinsville and also claimed Union General W.F. "Baldy" Smith took his farm in October 1861 for the quartering of horses and troops, cutting all the timber of his farm, shade and fruit trees to open the view for the cannon range for Camp Griffin. His fences were also taken, mainly used for fuel but also for building stables and quarters. He claimed the value of his farm was further decreased by the roads made through his property: "The farm was badly cut up by driving teams across. The winter was very wet and open, and the Teamsters drove where they could find the driest land."[108]

Henry Escridge was a free colored man and also lived near Lewinsville during the war. "I was resident at Mr. Swinks. I was working on the Leesburg Turnpike. I resided on the same farm during the war, worked part of it for three years. The rest of the time I was chopping and working about. I took the U.S. [side]. I had no vote. I had not much to say but I told those to whom I had a right to speak to stand to the Government. I understood if the rebels succeeded they were going to make all free persons of color slaves."[109] General W.F. "Baldy" Smith took Escridge's corn in October 1861. "It was an elegant crop of corn. Vermont soldiers took it all in one day. There was about 32 wagons."

Ferdinand Seals was a slave during the war who provided a deposition for Escridge: "I used to go near the Union Camp and set on the fence for fear the rebels would come and take me away, and Henry used to bring victuals to me. I was a slave man, and Henry was a free man. I was sure they [the Confederates] would take me off if they came." Seals belonged to Billy Swinks. Although Seals lived at the Swinks's house during most of the war, at the beginning of the war he was concerned about being near the Confederates, saying, "I must go away from here. I have been sold often enough, and I am going to leave."

The civilians of Langley filed a large number of claims about their treatment during the war. Their property and land was also allegedly taken by General "Baldy" Smith. Susanna Storm, the widow of Alonzo Storm, filed a claim stating General Smith's division camped in the neighborhood near Chain Bridge in September 1861. She charged Smith with ordering his captains to take cattle, oats, corn and hay. The corn was noted as "not ripe, but fit for roasting and for forage."[110]

Henry A. Lockwood lived near Langley and was a government worker in Washington. He lived mostly in Washington because "of trouble getting passes." Apparently, the provost marshal in Fort Ethan Allen did not get up very early so, "I found it necessary in order to be at the Department here, as I ought to be, I found it necessary to leave there [Langley] and come to the city."[111] His sister lived on Lockwood's farm and saw the fence taken down by pickets in the fall of 1861. She reported they were used to build "little picket houses" for the soldiers of Fort Ethan Allen, less than a half mile away. She "saw soldiers carry away potatoes and garden stuff." She also reported soldiers "broke open the house and took away a hundred dollars worth of furniture. They took away and killed a very valuable sow and took about 75 nice large hens."

Thomas J. Carper lived at Prospect Hill near Langley. He claimed to have voted for the Union and did so at Lewinsville. He also asserted that he gave Union General

James Samuel Wadsworth the name of a Confederate spy, who was subsequently arrested. Unlike Henry Lockwood, he received passes from the provost marshal at Fort Ethan Allen and was allowed to go to Washington.[112] He was also allowed to carry arms to protect himself, as he was continually threatened by Rebels.

In his absence in the fall of 1861, one witness claimed a Confederate Captain Hatcher threatened to burn Carper's house, but was persuaded against it by a Confederate sympathizer. The Rebel told the captain his own house would be burned in turn by Union troops in retaliation. Another witness for Carper claimed oats, fodder, corn and hogs were taken by two to three hundred Union troops on the march to Balls Bluff in October.[113] A witness claimed to have seen the soldiers carrying the fodder from the field "in their arms." They also burned fence rails of chestnut and oak for cooking, noting, "They were very good rails."

One of Carper's former slaves recounted, "I was formerly the slave of Mr. Carper and I am working for him now. I am not in his debt. He advised me to flee to Washington to keep me from being taken south and afterwards advised me to get employment from the government and I did. When General McCall's Division came, the hogs were in the field. The soldiers went into the same field and I heard the hogs squealing and after the soldiers left I remember seeing two or three skins of the hog. There were ten in the fields altogether. I don't remember seeing any hogs after the soldiers left."

Aaron Oliver also lived near Prospect Hill. He voted against the Ordinance of Secession. "I was a voter, and did vote the day they [Union troops] went to Alexandria, the day Ellsworth was killed. I voted against the ordinance in [Lewinsville] Fairfax County. I was ordered to be arrested because I held my loyalty. I had three different [Confederates] come there to get my fowls and give cash for them, but I don't see how I could have sold these fowls to them & yet maintain my loyalty. That was my impression then, and is now. They threatened to arrest me because I would not sell fowls, and I informed the Provost Marshall of it and he let them know if they arrested me he would arrest their citizens in my place, and therefore the citizens let me alone."[114]

Perry Elliott lived in Langley. He made numerous trips to Washington, "Twice to keep out of the way of rebels." After meeting General "Baldy" Smith he received a pass to travel to the market in Washington. He talked about the problems living in the area. He was "never arrested by Confederates, but was arrested by United States soldiers. They came to my house at night, I got up, and they arrested me, and carried me to Fort Marcy, about a quarter of a mile from my house. They said someone fired on their pickets. They kept me until nearly eleven o'clock [the] next morning when the Colonel came, and I was released."[115]

He was told "he would have to leave the country" by Secessionists who threatened him because "he would not got over on their side. I voted at the Lewinsville Precinct. I was the first one to vote against the ordinance. I voted for the Union and stuck to it."[116]

Martha Corbin Ball lived at Prospect Hill but died in 1865. Her heirs made a $54,000 claim for the following property destroyed during the war: "23,000 cords

CONTRABANDS COMING INTO THE FEDERAL

Slaves or "Contrabands of War" seeking refuge at a Union camp, circa 1863. *Fairfax County Public Library, Photographic Archives.*

AMP IN VIRGINIA. — FROM A SKETCH BY EDWIN FORBES.

of oak wood; 8,000 cords of pine wood; 3 dwellings, 3 stables, outbuildings, and quarters; 3,000 panels of fencing." Her administrator, although not listed as a claimant, was none other than Mottram Dulaney Ball, organizer of the Confederate Fairfax Cavalry and her son. In his deposition, however, he only identified himself as M.D. Ball.[117] Although there were 18 dispositions in her claim, the Southern Claims Commission filed a rare Summary Report explaining their decision in this particular case:

> *Mrs. Martha Ball, who died since the war, and whose property is alleged to have been taken in her life-time, was an aged lady, and seems to have [been] under control of her son who was not a loyal man. At all events, she went with him from the Union side to the Confederate side of the lines during the war. There is some testimony of the family to loyal expressions, but nothing decisive or satisfactory as to the real sentiments and position of the claimant. The matter was referred to Special Agent Tucker, who took the testimony of several witnesses, from which it seems that claimant's sympathies, like those of her numerous family and relatives, were with the south. With the positive testimony to establish loyalty, we are constrained to reject the claim.*

The citizens of Falls Church had their share of stories as well during the first year of the war. One resident described the village of Falls Church containing about two hundred residents. "There were only two families in the Village that were rebels."[118]

Catherine Ann Minor's claim after the war for reparations was rejected because she did not own the property for which she made a claim. The claims commission noted she only had a life interest in the property.[119] Nicholas Lemon, who provided a deposition for her, talked about being forced to vote for Secession against his will:

> *I voted for Secession* [at Falls Church] *under durance vile: under a threat. I came here to Washington on the day of the election with the determination not to go to the poles for fear of their being a row there, being a peaceable man, and on my way home just about sundown when I had escaped the trouble I met some of my neighbors. They told me there was a threat out for me, that if I did not go to the pole, and vote for Secession I would have to leave the state and that probably I would not get out very safe. I was so unaccustomed to anything of the kind, that I confess I was very much intimidated and under those circumstances I voted.*[120]

The brother of Mrs. Minor's husband also provided a deposition. He lived next to Mrs. Minor before the war but moved to Washington once the war began. "The armies were stationed on each side of me, the Confederates on one side and the federals on the other, within one quarter mile of each other, and I was between the two and they were firing. I wanted to find a more quiet place, so I came to Washington."

Another woman in Falls Church, Mary E. Martin, married a Union soldier during the war:

After [the] first battle of Bull Run the rebel army came down [to Falls Church] and took possession. The rebels abuse me and said I had taken sides with the Union. I left my home and went up to Upton's hill and there I met the Union forces coming up. This was about four weeks after the battle. The Union forces then advanced to Falls Church and I went home. I gave the Union army my house as a hospital. I have given victuals to the sick in the hospital. In August 1862 I married Edward Martin. He was a private soldier in the 22nd New York. He had been discharged in March 1862. In July 1863 he enlisted in a Massachusetts regiment, the number I never ascertained. He went away. I never saw him afterwards but I heard from soldiers afterwards that he got killed in the battle of the Wilderness. I never got any bounty or pension. [121]

Adam Martin of Falls Church described the men of a New York regiment under Colonel Corrigan who camped near his house in Falls Church, "The men were rough and fighting among themselves."[122]

William Sherman voted against the ratification of the ordinance in Lewinsville where Secessionists were similarly rough on Union supporters.[123] He came close to being beaten for expressing his views.

A man by the name of Ashford struck me two or three times in the head. This happened in Washington shortly after Mr. Lincoln was elected. We got to talking about the elections. He said that grand scoundrel Lincoln was elected. That he was born in the ashes and raised in the ashes. I told him Mr. Lincoln was not my choice before he was elected but that after his election he was my choice. Ashford wanted to know how that was. I told him because Mr. Lincoln was the choice of the people, and I should support him. He then struck me. I turned upon him and blacked both his eyes. Upon other things he said Lincoln would free the niggers. I told him that would not hurt me. [124]

Falls Church residents were subject to being arrested by both sides. John William Lynch described how he

was arrested once by the rebels just after the first battle of Bull Run. [I] had gone down to Mr. Hatch, an old crippled man, to saw some wood for him. His place is about a quarter of a mile from mine, while I was there a rebel soldier came and arrested me and carried me before Captain Nelson. They kept me I suppose about three quarters of an hour and then Capt. Nelson told me to go home and remain there. They did not tell me why I was arrested.

I was arrested twice by the United States troops. The first time just after the second battle of Bull Run. They had posted a picket line on my place during the night & in the morning I started to go to my stable, which was outside of their picket line, but I did not know it. They halted me and detained me, about fifteen minutes, and then released me, but told me I must not cross the picket line. They took the picket line away that same day, and in about a weeks time put it back there. I was going to my stable, not knowing they had replaced the picket line, when they arrested me a second time, but soon released me when I told them I did not know their picket line was there. I was never arrested at any other time.[125]

Lynch also recounted how the Rebels threatened to burn his house after the first Bull Run fight: "There was a squad of rebel soldiers in the road, and the one made the threats, was in my corn field. I had ordered him out. He said I was no Southern man or I would not object to his getting corn."

Reuben Ives of Falls Church recounted how he fed the soldiers of the Union army on their return from the first battle of Bull Run.

The rebel army followed the next day. My family all left and went to the city with the Union army. I remained there [at home], *and before morning the rebel army came in, and put a guard around my place. They arrested and tried me and threatened to take me to Richmond, but finally allowed me to remain. Then the federal army came in again. But we were* [then] *troubled by the guerillas from the rebel army and we appealed to the government for assistance and Gen. Augur furnished me with arms and ammunition for which I became responsible and we organized a home guard. After the war closed I returned the arms.*[126]

Hugh W. Throckmorton lived at Upton's Hill just east of Falls Church. He claimed General Wadsworth's command camped on his property during the winter of 1861–1862 at what was originally called Fort Upton and then Fort Ramsey. His house was used as a hospital for a telegraph unit and signal station for the duration of the war. General Wadsworth used his parlor as his office and slept in the next room. Dr. Pineo, the brigade physician, used another room in Throckmorton's house. He stated that U.S. troops came across the Potomac River on May 24, 1861, and then several companies arrived on the Alexandria Loudoun and Hampshire railroad over the next three to four weeks to guard the railroad. When they ran out of provisions he provided them with flour, meat, meal and cooked for them. "The day after the battle of Bull Run I came away with my family and brought all I could with my teams, afterwards sent my teams to get some other tings, the rebels were lying in ambush, surrounded and captured the teams, took my drivers prisoner, and I lost my team and wagon."[127]

The construction of the fort caused great damage to his property. "The forts and earthworks covered three acres and mounted 13 thirty-two pounder guns. [The] fort was right in front of the house on the summit of Upton's Hill. They built up on the top of the house twenty feet more than the cupola I had there, for the purpose of mounting a large glass to take observation of the country with. They could see from my house right into Fairfax Court House and watch the movements of the Confederates there."

Two rooms in the house were used as a hospital during the winter of 1862 and two men died there. Throckmorton's attorney stated in his claim, "If Upton's Hill was not the place where the military forces operated at the seat of war, it would be very difficult to name such a place."

James E. Murray also lived on Upton's Hill. His story included his survival of fighting and the Confederates on Upton's Hill:

> Some ten or twelve days after the first battle of Bull Run, just about dark, I was standing on my porch. I had no idea there was any rebels about there that close. I was right between the two lines and the Union soldiers at Upton's Hill were skirmishing with the rebels that day. Some one in the bushes fires at me and the ball struck on the post of the porch.
>
> A man by the name of Andrew Allen was with me in the house getting supper. I told him I believed they were shooting at us. Just then the rebels began firing at Upton's house with cannon. I ran south of the house and got down into the hay barrack and hid myself. Allen came running to me and the rebels saw him and fired a whole volley at him and then [the Rebels] run to the hay barrack and found us both.
>
> I thought they were going to kill us they were so savage and said we were spies. They took us prisoner and carried us up to Falls Church that night under guard, and the next day sent us under guard to Fairfax Court House and put us in jail. That is, they made a jail of the courthouse.
>
> Before they put us in jail they took us before General Longstreet who sent for John Chichester who lived in Fairfax Court House and asked him if he knew us. He said that he did "and that he did not know any good of us." General Longstreet then ordered us to jail.
>
> They kept us there four or five days and then sent us to Manassas under guard along with four or five Union soldiers they had captured. We remained there until the last of September, 1861. At about that time one George Padgett came along who knew us. He asked me what I was there for. I told them I had been arrested and brought there and I had not seen the charges against me and did not know what they were. I told him I wanted to have a trial. He told me he would get a trial for me. Padgett did so, and [I] was released.[128]

In the meantime, the Rebels had taken Murray's horses, wagon, two hogs, his fowls and all the furniture from his house. General Wadsworth's camp was approximately three hundred yards from his house, so the soldiers took four tons of his hay for bedding and also cut the timber on the hill, as it obstructed the view from Fort Buffalo.

Frederick Foote, a colored farmer, also provided a deposition for Murray:

> I could stand in my door and call to him in his door. I never belonged to him or lived on his land. I was emancipated some time before the war. I was always for

Camp Knox,

The Camp of the 4th Maine Vols. in

Situated on Lawson's Hill, on the Fairfax Road, 2 1-2 mile

he winter of 1861=62,

rom Alexandria, Va.

A typical camp among the civilian population. *Fairfax County Public Library, Photographic Archives.*

A view of Mount Vernon from the Potomac River as many soldiers witnessed it during the war.
Charles V. Mauro.

> *the Union. I could not be any other way. I remember he told me one evening when he and I was lying in the grass in the spring, that if the state of Virginia seceded we would all have to leave. He said to me "Frederick if Virginia secedes this will be no place for a poor white man or a free colored man. We will have to leave. The rich men will drive us away." I went north with General Tyler of the Conn. Brigade after the battle of Bull Run.*

Others on Upton's Hill feared both the Confederate and Union soldiers drawn to that advantageous high ground. Union General Tyler arrested every citizen along the telegraph line to his headquarters on the hill after it was cut. Others feared the Confederates would cut a hole in the roof of their house to use it as a signal station.[129]

Another colored man who lived on Upton's Hill was a carpenter named Gabriel Jones who lived with his sisters on his brother's farm. He was born free. During the war he worked on the fortifications that provided the defenses around Washington and was also a cook for the Union soldiers. He stated, "If rebels had built fortifications [and paid him], he would not have worked for them." Jones was never a friend to the Rebels. "They kept us down so long, and I was afraid of them to tell you the truth about it. I pretty much knew a good many of them and I knew their principles and what they were trying to do. I was just what you may call free, and they wanted to make me real down in bondage, but I liked freedom above all things."

General Wadsworth's men took wood from the property on which Jones lived. "When we came out to cut wood the [Union] soldiers used to pretty much stop there as it was the only convenient place. Mosby and most of the folks around here wanted to get us broke up, and they came in and took two of my sisters and two or three children in the night and then they ransacked the house but I got out. I got out of the way and they ransacked the house and took all what little money I had and all the papers and destroyed everything. I pounced out and just saved myself and that was all." Jones never knew where the children were taken "but they got back since."

Daniel F. Dulaney stated that Jones had rented land from his mother before the war. When asked by the commission why he had rented land from a known Rebel, Jones replied, "Well, a couple of years before the war you know we couldn't tell."

The armies had arrived in Fairfax County during the first year of the war, but the civilian suffering was just beginning.

One of the few properties that escaped the depredations brought by the war was one of the few that the soldiers on both sides respected. Although it was located directly between the two warring armies, soldiers only visited Mount Vernon as tourists. In 1858 the estate had been sold to the Mount Vernon Ladies' Association, which raised funds to restore the ill-kept mansion. Soldiers were only allowed to visit in small groups, could not wear their military uniforms and had to pay the standard twenty-five cents admission after stacking their arms before entering. Confederate soldiers did not visit the estate after the war began. Union soldiers, however, took advantage of their once-in-a-lifetime opportunities throughout the conflict to visit the estate as it was considered a national shrine on "sacred soil."[130]

Major Battles

By the beginning of 1862, the Confederate army was in winter quarters in Centreville in western Fairfax County, and the Union army quartered in the fortifications built throughout eastern Fairfax County.

The 40,000 Confederate troops in Centreville under General Joe Johnston certainly overwhelmed the small village, with its population of fewer than 220. The town, however, had its strategic value for the Confederates, due to its proximity to the Orange and Alexandria and Manassas Gap Railroads and its height on the Warrenton Turnpike, twenty-seven miles from Washington. Interestingly, the village's original name of Newgate had changed to Centreville in 1792 denoting the town's central position between Leesburg, Middleburg, Warrenton, Washington, Georgetown and Alexandria.[131]

The Confederate army constructed over five miles of earthworks and used all available fields for drill grounds. Their need for lumber for housing and firewood overwhelmed the resources of the area as 1,500 log cabins had been built by the end of 1861. One local resident spoke of the winter of 1861 to 1862: "There was enough firewood on our farm to last us hundreds of years. But during the winter the southern troops had their winter quarters there and cut down every last bit of it, built log houses to live in and they even used our logs to corduroy the road from Centreville to Manassas. And all during the winter they burned our trees for firewood. We were beginning to worry what we were going to do for wood for ourselves the next winter."[132]

On the other end of the county, Union soldiers on Upton's Hill were awakened at morning reveille by the "Sounds From Home" by a unit band after they had serenaded

General Wadsworth on New Year's Eve. In Falls Church, most Union soldiers spent the first New Year of the war on the quiet side, refraining from marching or parading. Later in the day, the soldiers enjoyed a greased-pig chase. "The piggies were escorted with all due pomp and ceremony, with horns trumpeting, drums beating, and regimental colors flying, to a nearby field for the festivities. After which the men dined on pork."[133]

Chalky Gillingham "entertained" three Union officers and two privates for dinner on his farm near Mount Vernon on New Year's Day after hauling wood out of the swamp on a day he described as "warm and pleasant as spring." During the month of January, Gillingham reported in his journal that fifteen thousand Union infantry and cavalry were camped within four miles of his farm.[134]

Gillingham with the other Quakers in the area had built a meetinghouse on the Woodlawn Plantation in 1853, called it the Woodlawn Meetinghouse and held monthly, quarterly, half-yearly and yearly meetings. The soldiers in the area used the meetinghouse for their headquarters. Regiments of one thousand soldiers performed

Confederate quarters showing the need for wood built in Centreville during the winter of 1861–1862. *Fairfax County Public Library, Photographic Archives.*

local picket duty for three days at a time. Gillingham complained of the destruction and filthy conditions that the soldiers left in the meetinghouse. On days that they were not using the meetinghouse, Gillingham and other members of the Friends cleaned up: "Most of the members went to the Meeting house and cleaned it; the soldiers having left it very dirty. The floor could not be seen for the dirt. We carried the benches out and scrubbed them and put two coats of whitewash on the house. I spent the next day there also, repairing windows and drying the house." That night the soldiers returned and "made the floor and benches as dirty as ever. They cut the nice new smooth benches for kindling wood."[135]

Farther north in the county, Union officers preferred to spend the winter in the now-closed Episcopal Seminary. The seminary provided such good quarters that many officers invited their wives to live there with them. They enjoyed the carpeted rooms with a stove in each and "all the comforts of home." Unfortunately, the soldiers took liberty with the contents left in the school. They took artworks and instruments of both

Union soldiers occupying Secessionist Bill Taylor's Tavern on Taylor Hill in Falls Church, circa 1862. *Fairfax County Public Library, Photographic Archives.*

the musical and scientific varieties for themselves. Some even took the clothes left by the professors. The books in the school library had to be removed to warehouses and the Smithsonian Institution for safekeeping. In a rare decision to respect the property of the local civilians, Union General William B. Franklin and his staff refused to occupy citizens' homes and spent the winter in tents.[136]

Over the first two months of the year, Union soldiers continued to occupy the eastern areas of the county including Falls Church, Taylor's Hill, Wilton Hill, Upton's Hill, Flint Hill, Hunter's Mill, Minor's Hill, Langley and Vienna.

Many of the civilians learned what they could of the outside world through the few newspapers they could find, and those newspapers came from the Union soldiers in the camps in their midst.[137]

In March, a major change was about to take place that would alter the makeup of the troops that occupied Fairfax County for the rest of the war. Confederate General Joe Johnston met with President Jefferson Davis and his cabinet in Richmond in mid-February and decided that their defensive position in Centreville was weak, should McClellan advance with one hundred thousand men against Johnston's forty thousand.[138]

On February 22, Johnston ordered the removal of the Confederate food supplies at Manassas Junction. Johnston would remove three million pounds of food and provisions. Unfortunately, he could not carry it all. In a brief bonanza, the local civilians were allowed to take whatever they could of one million pounds of stores before the Confederates put it to the torch. Upon leaving, the Confederates destroyed the stone bridge over Bull Run on the Warrenton Turnpike using five hundred pounds of gunpowder.[139]

As the Confederate army left Centreville, they moved into new camps south of the Rappahannock River in central Virginia on March 13. On the same day, Union troops had rushed across Fairfax County and moved into the newly vacated positions in Centreville. McClellan, after finding nothing but a sea of red mud, left a small guard at Centreville and ordered the Union army back to the fortifications in eastern Fairfax County. The major threat to Washington was now gone.[140]

As the Confederates left Barnes's Mill at Hope Park in March, Union soldiers advanced into western Fairfax County on foraging expeditions, taking what supplies they needed from the civilians. At Hope Park, they confiscated all they could carry, including vegetables and pigs. One of the pigs taken, however, belonged to ten-year-old Nettie Barnes, and she was not about to let the Union soldiers take her very own pig. The family story is told as follows:

> *Nettie carried on so that mama finally told one of the slaves to take her over to the camp and see if the Union soldiers wouldn't give the pet pig back. The two were met by sentries, who took Nettie and the servant before the commander. Nettie, between sobs, told about the theft of her pig and pleaded for its return.*
>
> *The Yankee officer asked Nettie if she could point out the soldier who had taken her pig. She said she could. So the officer lined up the raiding company up in front of Nettie*

and she quickly picked out the guilty one. The officer didn't order the man shot, but he did order him to return the pig post-haste. The soldier saluted, got the pig and carried it back to our home, with Nettie and the servant trudging along beside him.[141]

Along with their withdrawal from Centreville, the Confederates also retreated from Fairfax Court House, leaving the crossroads in early spring to Union hands for the rest of the war. The area provided them a key point of communication and supplies for the rest of the war. The courthouse area became a Union military outpost and minor headquarters in the defense of Washington. This area, as well as the rest of the county, would not remain dormant, however, as hostilities would "smolder in Northern Virginia," stoked by the irregular troops left behind. Many of the innocent-looking farmers in western Fairfax County and counties farther west put on Confederate uniforms at night and attacked isolated Union outposts, supply lines, bridges and communications centers for the rest of the war.[142]

Bands of guerillas kept thousands of Union troops on guard duty throughout the county and fighting skirmishes on an almost daily basis. Civil War historian Bruce Catton described these guerillas as follows: "The quality of these bands varied greatly. At the top was John S. Mosby's courageous soldiers led by a minor genius, highly effective in partisan warfare. Most of the groups, however, were about one degree better than plain outlaws, living for loot and excitement, doing no actual fighting if they could help it, and offering a secure refuge to any number of Confederate deserters and draft evaders. The worst damage which this system did to the Confederacy, however, was that it put Yankee soldiers in a mood to be vengeful."[143] The Yankees were vengeful, no doubt, to suspected guerillas and also to the civilians in the county who protected them or were deemed to be Southern sympathizers.

The next change in the troops in Fairfax County would be decided on March 13 at a council of corps commanders at Fairfax Court House now under McClellan. A waterborne Union plan for spring operations was approved to attack Richmond via the peninsula between the York and James Rivers. The result would be movement south of 150,000 soldiers, 15,000 horses, 1,100 wagons and 44 batteries from Washington and the surrounding vicinity.[144] After the major buildup of troops in the county in 1861, the Confederates left Fairfax first in the spring of 1862, followed by most of the Union soldiers.

The Fourth Vermont left camp near Lewinsville on March 10 and marched west toward Manassas as the Confederates were leaving Centreville. They stopped at Flint Hill, north of Fairfax Court House, before turning east on March 15 as McClellan changed his plans and started his troops toward Richmond via the wharfs at Alexandria. The Fourth Vermont marched to Cloud's Mill, northeast of Alexandria, before finally moving into Alexandria and boarding transports to take them south for the Peninsula Campaign.[145]

Chalky Gillingham noted in his journal that he saw fifty thousand to sixty thousand Union troops "embarking for some point south" via fifty or more steamboats on March 26 from Alexandria.[146]

The courthouse at Fairfax in Union hands showing both civilians and soldiers, 1863. *Fairfax County Public Library, Photographic Archives.*

The village of Lewinsville under Union control, 1861. *Fairfax County Public Library, Photographic Archives.*

In a rare reversal of the usual behavior of troops taking what they wanted, Captain W.A. Hawley and Lieutenant Colonel W.B. Hazmand of the 102nd New York Volunteer Battalion left all army materials to Jacob Smoot, the owner of Salona in Langley, when the Union troops moved out of Camp Griffin for the trip toward Richmond on March 24.[147]

Anne Frobel recorded her impressions of the Union soldiers who left her property as well. She had recorded rumors in her diary in early March that the whole army was to make a great move and that preparations had started to be made. On March 17, she noted that "they broke camp here and marched off to Alex—there to take ship for the Peninsula and O with what thankful hearts did we watch their departure." After the troops left, Anne

went to town (presumably Washington) and described the sight: "The Potomac River from Wa[shington] city to the effort, as far as we could see was one solid mass of white canvas. You could only get glimps of the water here and there so thickly were the vessels, boats, steamers, little and big, of all sizes and shapes, crowded, crowded, packed together."[148]

Although she hoped for a better situation when she returned home, she discovered not all the Union soldiers had gone, as new soldiers had come to occupy her house. "I could not give them a hearty welcome, for beside their being yankees, we were getting very scarce of provisions, and the restrictions in getting to town, or getting anything from there makes it very difficult at times to find enough to feed our own family. I don't know what we shall do."[149]

Even though the main bulk of the Army of the Potomac was indeed moving south toward Richmond, the defense of Washington was of equal importance. Brigadier

Camp Griffin, a Union training and supply depot at Salona, circa 1862. *Fairfax County Public Library, Photographic Archives.*

General James Wadsworth was ordered to move all troops north of Washington south across the Potomac into Northern Virginia. The troops totaled 35,000 under Major General Nathaniel Banks in the Shenandoah, close to 11,000 at Manassas, almost 8,000 at Warrenton, 1,350 on the lower Potomac and 18,000 under Wadsworth in Washington and in Fairfax County.[150]

These troops found little to do during the summer except drill, march between forts and practice their artillery. In Alexandria, General John P. Slough became the military governor. Slough arrived to find an utter lack of order. Both civilians and soldiers were drunk in the streets and at the docks. Robberies, rioting and murders were running rampant. The rest of the civilian population in Alexandria dared not leave their houses for fear of life and property. Slough banned the sale of liquor in restaurants and bars and instituted a curfew. The soldiers of the Thirty-fourth Massachusetts and other regiments promptly disobeyed these orders, raiding local vegetable gardens nightly.[151]

When McClellan's unsuccessful Peninsula Campaign was concluded, he returned to Alexandria on August 26, followed by his troops. The streets were choked by army wagons. The Potomac River was crowded with returning ships, and the wharves strained under the weight of the incoming army material. Commercial business thrived again after the summer interlude as the soldiers devoured any food other than salt beef and hardtack and "dealers discovered that soldiers would buy anything that flashed, glittered or was plated."[152]

In the meantime, President Lincoln had formed the Army of Virginia under Major General John Pope from the forces under Generals Fremont, Banks and McDowell totaling close to fifty thousand men. They would be ordered to Manassas Junction from Warrenton on August 27 and then on to Manassas to meet the threat from Confederate General Thomas "Stonewall" Jackson leading to the Second Battle of Manassas on August 29 and 30.[153]

Elements of the army under Major Generals Joseph Hooker, Philip Kearny and Irvin McDowell moved through Centreville on the twenty-eighth before engaging at Manassas the following two days. Having returned from the Peninsula Campaign, Union General William B. Franklin moved through Annandale with ten thousand men of the Sixth Corps on his way to Manassas after being delayed due to the lack of wagons in Alexandria. Franklin only reached Centreville on August 30, too late to get involved in Manassas's second major battle. The sounds of the cannon signaling the Union army's defeat at the Battle of Second Manassas could be heard as far east as Mount Vernon, Falls Church and Alexandria.[154]

The retreat by the Union army east to the defenses around Washington would lead to the only major battle fought in the county. On the evening of August 30, Major General John Pope ordered the retreat of forty thousand men of the Union army east from Manassas along the Warrenton Turnpike, today's Route 29, across a wood repaired Stone Bridge into the heights of Centreville.[155]

On the morning of the following day, Confederate General Robert E. Lee decided to attempt to position a portion of his army between Centreville and Fairfax Court House in order to bring the Union army into battle before they could reach the formidable defenses in eastern Fairfax County and Washington. To do so, he ordered the fifteen to twenty thousand men of "Stonewall" Jackson's wing to march north from Manassas on Gum Springs Road and then turn east on the Little River Turnpike, today's Route 50, in the attempt to reach the intersection of the two turnpikes at Germantown, just west of the courthouse.[156]

On September 1, both armies were traveling east across Fairfax County, the Confederate troops on the Little River Turnpike to the north and the Union troops on the Warrenton Turnpike to the south, approaching an inevitable collision. Pope, now receiving reports of the Confederate flanking movement, sent patrols out to report on the whereabouts of the Confederates. At 2:00 p.m., the Union Ninth Corps, led by Major General Isaac Stevens, received orders to move east from Centreville and move north toward the Little River Turnpike. Following a local guide, they turned north on a cart path from the Warrenton Turnpike, just short of their intended path up the Ox Road.[157]

By the time the Union troops reached their destination along the Little River Turnpike, Jackson, who was also aware of the Union army's possible attempt to intercept him, had already decided to hold at the area where the Ox Road crossed the Little River Turnpike, known as Ox Hill. When the two thousand men under Stevens's command came up to the Little River Turnpike, Stevens sent his men forward while sending back a messenger for reinforcements, which he would desperately need if he was to stop the advance of Jackson's wing.

At 4:00 p.m., in order to protect his army's line of retreat, Stevens attacked the Confederate forces on both sides of the Ox Road—today's West Ox Road, just south of the Little River Turnpike (today's Route 50). After an hour of fighting, Stevens was killed while leading his men into a Confederate line of troops. His reinforcements of 1,500 men under Brigadier General David Birney reached the battlefield and went into battle alongside Stevens's troops. A heavy thunderstorm broke across the field at the time of Stevens's death.[158]

Major General Philip Kearny also reached the battlefield and, attempting to ascertain the situation in the dark and under heavy rain, accidentally rode into Confederate troops and was killed while riding away in a muddy cornfield at 6:15 p.m. At 6:30 p.m., rain and darkness completed the effort Stevens had started to halt the progress of the Confederate army, and both armies pulled back from the Little River Turnpike and went into bivouac for the night. Confederate General James Longstreet and his wing reached the battlefield that evening too late to join in the action.[159]

The following morning, Lee would find that the Union army had moved past him and completed their retreat to the defenses and substantial fortifications surrounding Washington. His attempt to intercept Pope's army had failed. The Confederate army claimed victory, however, as they held the battlefield. Lee could not sustain his army to attack Washington in the desolate area of Fairfax County, so he turned north into Maryland and met the Union army again, this time at the battles of South Mountain and Antietam on September 14 and 17.[160]

The Battle of Chantilly, as the Union army called it, or Ox Hill as the Confederates named it, Fairfax County's only major battle, lasted two and one half hours with 270

Confederate Partisan Ranger John Singleton Mosby. *Herndon Historical Society.*

men killed, 1,125 wounded and 105 captured. Following their second defeat in a matter of days, General McClellan replaced Pope as the commander of both Union armies, now termed the Army of the Potomac, on September 2.[161]

Three thousand wounded Union soldiers from both Second Manassas and Chantilly were evacuated south along the eastern portion of the Ox Road, today's Route 123, to Fairfax Station. There, they were cared for in part by Clara Barton before being loaded onto cars and transported to Alexandria via the Orange and Alexandria Railroad.[162] The civilians in the county had now seen a major battle and its horrendous effects close up, as civilians discovered remains in shallow graves in the days following the battle.

All the available public spaces in Falls Church were crowded with wounded who poured into Falls Church after the battles at Manassas and Chantilly. Local women were pressed into service to act as nurses in makeshift hospitals.[163]

The 104th New York retreated from Centreville to Falls Church and on to Arlington Heights. Soldiers on duty on Upton's Hill were on high alert for pursuing Confederates.[164]

Union soldiers, no matter on the run, still found time to take whatever they wanted as they raced through the town. German soldiers ransacked Reuben Ives's home in Falls Church taking all his furniture, his bedding and blankets and even his clock for use in their camp at Fort Buffalo. Being hungry, they killed and took one of Ives's hogs. The soldiers, having been on short rations for days while fighting, also stripped the interior of Lewis Crump's house, as well as his hog and chickens, which they killed, cooked and ate while at his house.[165]

Talmadge Thorn of Falls Church encountered a different problem:

> *At the time of Pope's retreat I got in the wake of Lee and they arrested me, and when they brought me up to Lee he asked me what flag I stood under, and I told him the stars and stripes. I told Lee that and he said "You must go with me." From there I went to Richmond, and I was about ten days going and I was there from the 28th of August, when I was captured, until I was paroled the 28th of March. I was in Libby prison part of the time, and part of the time in a prison they called "Castle Lightning."*[166]

While some Confederate troops pursued the retreating Union soldiers to Fairfax Court House, the Fifteenth Alabama Regiment left the Chantilly battlefield over the two days following the battle and moved west through Loudoun County, wading across the Potomac at White's Ford and on to Frederick, Maryland.[167]

Following the tactical draw at Antietam and Lee's retreat, President Lincoln signed the Emancipation Proclamation, freeing all the slaves in the Confederacy, including Virginia, on January 1, 1863. Visiting Alexandria, Anne Frobel noticed the hundreds and thousands of contrabands packed into the city, starving and destitute, smallpox killing them off in great numbers. Among the fugitive slaves in the Washington and Fairfax County area, the proclamation "brought a wave of rejoicing." The *Alexandria Gazette* reported the freed slaves "are holding meetings, and having a fine time generally, over the Proclamation. Singing, praying, shouting, speeches are the order of the day."[168]

The rest of the year in the county would see additional forts built, along with the reinforcement of existing ones. The number of Union soldiers would increase in Fairfax County as they returned through Alexandria from the outskirts of Richmond. Skirmishing would continue almost daily throughout the county.

First Lieutenant John Singleton Mosby served with Major General J.E.B. Stuart at Second Manassas and would become an independent partisan leader on December 31, 1862.[169] This one decision would haunt the Union soldiers in the county and surrounding area for the rest of the war.

Union General Heintzelman inspected the camps and forts at Upton's and Munson's Hills on September 26 amid constant Confederate activity in the area. Camp Cromwell was established for additional defense on Minor's Hill the same day.[170]

By the end of 1862, Washington was a well-defended city. Fifty-three forts and twenty-two batteries stood on Northern Virginia soil. Union pickets stretched westward from Fairfax Court House, Fairfax Station and Dranesville to Centreville.[171]

As the Union army settled into winter quarters for the second time during the war, some women turned to making a living as best they could. In Alexandria, prostitution became a nuisance to the residents but had plenty of customers from sedentary soldiers.[172]

Much of the weather at Fairfax Court House was reported as fine in December. Soldiers from Vermont recorded their service during the winter months "was not particularly exciting, the only enemy being guerrillas, the Confederate Mosby began operating in that quarter with his rangers."[173]

One soldier from Vermont recorded a name for the civilians in the area of the courthouse, calling any white landowner who had not taken the oath of allegiance to the United States an "FFV," or a member of a First Families of Virginia. In his reference, the soldier noted how a destitute farmer offered to haul and cut firewood for the Union pickets if they would leave his fences alone, as it was far easier to cut and carry firewood than to split and repair wood for fences.[174]

The officers stayed warm in log huts, while the soldiers were shivering from the coming cold winter nights and storms in their canvas tents. Union General Stoughton "added to the usual battalion drills, frequent brigade drills, for which the broad open plain near Fairfax Court House afforded admirable ground. A brigade band of 17 pieces furnished music for dress parades and special occasions. The camps were clean and orderly, the men well behaved, the health of the brigade was fair, and the time passed not unpleasantly."[175]

In the spring of 1862, the toll on civilians continued from the buildup that had occurred during the second half of 1861. Edwin C. Fitzhugh witnessed General "Baldy" Smith's men take the brick from the foundation of a vacant house on his property located on the Little River Turnpike between Alexandria and Fairfax Court House.[176] The men took the bricks from the cellar of his house and used them to make floors in their tents at Fort Worth. One soldier was badly hurt when the house collapsed. The soldiers continued to haul the bricks away in their wagons from the two-story brick house that also had a brick extension, a brick foundation for a porch and four brick chimneys for a period of six months. "All the material of the house was taken except for one dormer window which I got myself."

Robert Strong, who lived a half-mile northeast of Fairfax Court House on a hundred-acre dairy farm, also had a house taken as McClellan's troops moved into the area after the Confederates withdrew in the spring. "They made flooring [from the house] in their tents and doors to their tents. They had quite a little town built up and it was a beautiful place, and spring water, and plenty of wood, and there was a hill there from which they could look all over the country. It didn't take them long to take down the building. They were all wanting to build quarters and every one wanted to get a certain share of it."[177]

Uriah Ferguson claimed a supply train didn't arrive for General Blenker's troops on March 10, so the soldiers took provisions from his property in Fairfax Court House to their camp.[178]

Ambrose Cock's house was burned in the spring so the Union forces could see the Rebels at Annandale Church. The house was burned at four in the morning. General Blenker of the Eighth New York gave the family twenty minutes to vacate the premises and Cock was arrested and sent to jail. A neighbor testified, "Some beer-drinking Captain arrested him and sent him to Alexandria, and he was put in jail and kept there 2 or 3 days before I got him out. I believe the Captain stole some of his horses and that was the excuse for the arrest."[179]

Lucretia C. Merry's troubles began in January when General "Baldy" Smith's men took her fences to blockade the road from the Leesburg Pike to Lewinsville. In March, General McCall's division camped on her farm near Falls Church. Generals Meade and Orr used her house as their headquarters. Troops in her area had advanced to Hunter's Mill and returned to her farm. As it had been raining hard for two days, their supply train had not kept up with them. In a twenty-four-hour period, the troops took a sow and five pigs for General Porter's mess. The soldiers also took over two dozen hens, two barrels of corned beef of three hundred pounds each, twenty pounds of dried beef and ten bushels of potatoes. Some of the soldiers even cooked their meals in her kitchen. When she complained to an aide to General Meade, she was simply told, "The poor fellows had no rations."[180]

The same situation happened to Esther Ferguson near Fairfax Court House in March. It had been raining and the roads were very muddy, keeping the supply trains from reaching the troops located in her vicinity. General Blenker stayed at her house for two days, waiting for his supplies to arrive while his men killed her cows for food. Despite her treatment by the Union soldiers she claimed, "I never did anything for the rebels. They might have hung me but it would have done no good."[181]

A slave named John Thomas Bushrod had hay taken by Union soldiers on the White Marsh farm near Accotink, where he was working during 1862. When the war broke out, he was owned by David Fitzhugh but had been hired out to a Mr. Dainty. "I had sympathized with the Union cause. I once hurrahed for 'Uncle Abe' and Mr. Dainty struck me in the head for it. I loved the North and wanted freedom." After the Battle of First Bull Run, he moved to William Lee's White Marsh farm, where his wife worked for Lee. Union soldiers arrested Lee. As the owner was being taken away, Lee told

Bushrod to stay and take care of his place, and Bushrod could keep half of what he made. Bushrod stayed and worked the farm until the fall of Richmond. "I did not give half of what I raised but when [Lee] came back after the war I gave him some money and he was satisfied."[182]

As McClellan's men were returning from the Peninsula Campaign and just before Second Manassas, they took George W. Johnson's corn "out of the field by the bagful and the armful. They worked just like bees in a hive. They carried the corn to their camps. They were camped clear from Fort Lyon up to within two hundred yards from the cornfield," southeast of Alexandria on the Huntley Farm.[183]

Along Telegraph Road, even closer to Alexandria than Fort Lyon, Harvey J. Peck stated,

> *I have seen as many as ten or twelve* [soldiers] *at one time getting potatoes. They came to my house and got my hoes, and dug them and carried them away to their camp kettles. I asked them not to take my potatoes, but they said they were in need of them and must have them. After they told me that they were in want of them, I paid little attention to it, for I would have given the house I lived in to them of they had said they needed* [it]. *They were about two days taking them. There was less than a half acre of potatoes and they took the whole, I never harvested any.*[184]

Most of the claims from 1862 were made after the Union army's defeat at Second Manassas. They covered a wide area of the county. James Murtaugh in Centreville claimed to have had hay taken by General Hooker in August, just before the battle.

Jesse Harris was a black man who owned 263 acres near the Stone Bridge at Bull Run, as close as one could be to the Manassas battlefield and still live in Fairfax County. He was born free. "My mother was not [born free], but she was free before she had me." He was responsible for twenty children, as his wife already had nine children when he married her and they had eleven more together. Union forces took a colt and a mare, cattle and fifteen tons of hay: "I followed them the next morning and I got the colt but I could not get the mare. I couldn't get the cattle. I had six very large stacks of hay. They took every bit."[185]

Jesse's son, Obed, lived on a farm next to his father's. His father had helped him buy the forty-two-acre property. Like his father, he was born a free man, but his wife was a slave. Rebels had taken two of his best horses, all his hogs, geese and fowl. Obed kept what he could by hiding whatever he could from them. He was also raided by Union soldiers during the battle at Manassas, as he lived two miles east of the battlefield: "They were passing back and forward all the day and I laid 500 yards from the pike, and they were coming from the field to get something to eat. The government foragers took a couple of oxen. Only one man came to the house for them, but there was a colored man helped to drive them. I had them in the lot around the house to keep them out of the way and they drove them on the pike and he said he was going to carry them to the battle field. He said the men must have something to eat."[186] Obed did not follow to try to get his oxen back, as he was told there would no doubt be shooting.

Joseph Harris lived in Centreville where "there was a free settlement up in that neighborhood." The administrator of his claim described Harris as "a Union man and a very strong one, too. The Harrises generally had property; they were thrifty, industrious people. They were all free colored people before the war."

In his deposition to support Harris's claim, Charles Ratcliffe stated, "Joseph Harris belonged to my grandfather up to the time of my grandfather's death in February 9, 1854, who then set him free. He was a successful farmer, worked all day and half the night, one of the most industrious in that section for his age. He was in the neighborhood of 58 or 59." Pope's men destroyed Harris's crop of corn when they fell back after the Second Bull Run fight: "They camped in his field and staid two-thirds of a day and night. The corn was at its roasting-ear state and they had nothing to eat. They just took everything they could. They had no provisions and they just fed on them. Pope's army got some cattle. They killed two very fine veal calves." In an interesting comment on this former slave, Ratcliffe stated his grandfather set Harris free because Harris's "father had been a faithful foreman. I would like to see his children recover. His son is one of the best boys in Virginia."[187]

Betsey Johnson, who lived on the Poor House farm near Union Mills, was a freeborn black woman. She had property taken after Second Bull Run. Her husband, Benjamin, was a slave who lived with his master near Manassas in Prince William County when the war broke out. In the spring of 1862, he escaped from his master and went to live with his wife for the rest of the war. "The rebels took $150 in gold and silver from me, part was mine and part was my wife's. My wife had buried it in the ground and the rebels got after my little boy, and made him tell where it was. They asked him first if we had any money, and made him tell. The rebels were at Union Mills at this time. I never heard of the money any more."

Of the eight children they had, three of their sons were cooks in the Union army. Benjamin

washed clothing right smart for the Union Soldiers when they were at Union Mills. They paid me for it. My old boss, James H. Simpson, hired me out one month to [Confederate] *General Ewell. I staid one month with him. He gave me five dollars, and my master twelve dollars. I was cooking for Genl. Ewell, and did nothing else for him. I wanted the Union to gain the fight. My mistress told me to go south with her when the rebels fell back* [from Centreville in the spring of 1862]. *I told her I would stay where I was. Soon as I could I went to the Union side.*

The Rebels often told Betsey, "If they gained the day they would make all of us free blacks slaves. She rejoiced when the news came that Richmond had gone up."[188]

As General Pope retreated to Centreville after Second Manassas, Andrew Murtaugh's "place was covered with men, wagons, cattle, artillery, for four days, from Friday to Tuesday. Everything was in confusion. It makes my heart sick to think of it, to see so many wounded and suffering men, and not be able to do more for them. It seemed like everybody was lost or separated from their comrades, some had recently come from the

A lone civilian house along the Orange and Alexandria Railroad under the control of Union soldiers at
Union Mills in western Fairfax County. *Fairfax County Public Library, Photographic Archives.*

ls, Va.
dria R.R.

peninsula and had what they called the chickahominy fever. It was a sad sight." General Pope's headquarters was three quarters of a mile from his daughter.[189]

James M. Wells, who lived near Fairfax Court House, had his property covered with reserve corps soldiers after the Battle of Second Manassas. He had twenty acres of corn taken by General Gammell's Eighth Illinois Regiment, which was camped at the courthouse. New York mounted riflemen took an eight-year mare who was suckling a colt.[190]

John E. Febrey and his wife opened their house to the sick and wounded as they fell back through Falls Church the following fall and winter. The Febreys lived on Upton's Hill, where they tended to the sick of the 127th, 142nd, 143rd and 144th New York Regiments and a Massachusetts battery: "Mrs. Febrey gave her personal attention to those soldiers who were sick, and made broth and delicacies, and nursed them carefully."[191]

Most Union soldiers were used to taking whatever they wanted. The soldiers who camped on John William Lynch's place in Falls Church for six days took all the fencing that Lynch had rebuilt from the previous fall. There were so many soldiers on his property, Lynch vacated his house and returned only after the soldiers left.[192]

Soldiers took hay, potatoes, corn and a hog from Reuben Ives in Falls Church on their retreat as well. "They said they were hungry, [they] had been on short rations for several days, fighting and marching. There was no officer with them. They carried [the hog] off on a pole and went towards the camp." They also broke into his house and took clothing, bedding, blankets, flour and half a barrel of shad. "The house was broken open by a first Lieutenant, a German, who belonged to a New York regiment. After he left, the soldiers went in. I remonstrated with that officer and he used rather abusive language and paid no attention to me."[193]

Walter H. Erwin lived one hundred yards from John W. Lynch. A portion of General Wadsworth's troops camped on his place and "while there burned the fences around the house and garden. The traveling was very hard since the troops were in poor plight, some of them occupied our house and we made them as comfortable as we could. We were all ordered to leave the village as the place was to be burned, and we went to Washington for the night and came back the next day."[194]

The same plundering occurred in Annandale after Second Manassas. Isaac Haynes's house, barn and log barn were taken to Fairfax Court House by the quartermaster for the lumber. John Dougherty claimed, "The Vermont and N.Y. Cavalry took the corn, tore up the sheets to wrap up the wounded. A thousand soldiers were around the house and a good many wounded men. One man was shot through the neck. We made some mush and milk for him. He could eat nothing else."[195]

In the west end, Henry Clevenger suffered from Union soldiers going to and returning from Second Manassas. In June, two hundred head of government cattle ate a twelve-acre field of grass. In September the soldiers turned on a one-acre field of potatoes. "They dug them up with their bayonets and with their hands, and carried them off to their camps in haversacks. I guess they took them all within three weeks."[196]

Almond Birch, who lived west of Gum Spring, related how soldiers took his pigs: "I saw them take the pigs. They would come into the yard and put them on their bayonets. They were small pigs, and the larger ones they carried away."[197]

After Second Manassas and Chantilly, the major battles in and around Fairfax County were over for the remainder of the war. The occupation by Union soldiers, however, was not and the civilians continued to have their property taken, leaving less and less on which to subsist.

Charles Kirby of Fairfax Court House lost more of his property during the second year of the war. In September, he claimed that six hundred bushels of corn, two hundred bushels of potatoes and two hundred bushels of oats were taken by General Sigel's men. In December, he claimed Lieutenant Hitchings, the quartermaster of the Fortieth Massachusetts, took 140 cords of wood.[198]

William and Louisa Ferguson lived near Mount Vernon on Doag Run. They claimed the soldiers at Fort Lyon took a four-year-old sorrel horse with a foal in the winter of 1862. The Union soldiers broke into the stable and took the mare at night. William had been a slave; his wife, Louisa, was freeborn. Louisa stated, "All the secesh around there threatened me, and if our Union people had not come I am certain they would taken me and my children to Richmond." She had sixteen children. She claimed that her "father belonged to George Washington. He was Gen. Washington's carpenter. Gen. Washington set him free and my father afterwards bought my mother and set her free. I was born after my mother was set free." William belonged to Dennis Johnston and lived with his master until 1862, before escaping to his wife's farm.[199]

John W. Elgin of Clifton had problems with the Confederates early in the war. His horses were taken in the fall by General Sickles's corps. Three Confederates came one night after he had gone to bed: "I had a dog there and it jumped out, and the soldiers began acting badly; I run out and I says, 'Don't you hurt that dog!' and one of the soldiers took an oath and says, 'I'll cut you through and through you dam abolitionist!' My wife called me and says, 'John, come in here and don't talk with them at all.' But they kept on abusing me and finally passed on."

In 1862 Elgin had "not less than 100 soldiers at his house taking everything they could get hold of when they took the horses. They went to the stable, opened the door and took the horses and rode them off. I begged them not to use me so and told them I was not a Secessionist, but they would not believe me. Cows were taken from pasture in sight of the house. The soldiers killed them right on the place and dressed them and carried the meat off."[200]

Soldiers of the Fifth New York Regiment, stationed at Frying Pan just south of Herndon, took corn from Wesley Hall in the fall. Hall was allowed $199, and intelligence was apparently not required to collect on his claim. Unable to read, Hall had his statement read to him, being of "sluggish intellect." Isaiah Bready, who became Herndon's first mayor in 1879, stated Hall "was a poor man and before the war had worked at day's work, and was regarded as a man not altogether in his right mind. At time he would appear a little flighty."[201]

Samual Brown of Fairfax Court House claimed Union soldiers took four or six stacks of hay on September 1, the day of the Battle of Chantilly. Alexander Haight, who lived close to the Sully Plantation, saw the hay taken at Brown's farm. Haight and other local men frequently left for either Washington or Alexandria to keep from being arrested after hearing of a buildup of soldiers near their houses or the possibility of battles being fought nearby. They left their wives and families to protect their property. He described how he came to be at Samual Brown's farm on September 1: "That morning I was here in the city, and my family was at home on the place and I went out with a neighbor of mine expecting to get home (I didn't know of the retreat of the army) and I went to Gen. Wadsworth for a pass, but he could not give me any, but we went out and we met no pickets until we got to the forks of the road where Mr. Brown lives."[202]

Battlefields can be confusing to non-local participants, and the day after the Battle of Chantilly, a Union officer came to Nancy Worster's house in Chantilly and said he was lost, so "she told him where the Union line was."[203]

Confederate activity in the county was far from over. George W. Steele, who lived at Wolf Run Shoals in the western portion of the county, had continuing problems throughout the war. "When I voted against the ordinance of Secession John Marshall told me I ought to be shot." Steele's was the only vote against the ordinance in the Arundell precinct.[204] Lieutenant John Burke and six Confederates initially arrested him. In June 1861 "They came to my house and arrested me because they said I was disloyal to their government. Took me to Fairfax C.H. We reached there about noon. I was taken before Col. Moss. They accused me of going to Washington and carrying news. I told Col. Moss I had not been in Washington for 2 years. They kept me until night then released me."

In September 1862, the Rebels came to Steele's house around 10:00 p.m. and awoke him. They "told the family they were going to burn the house." His wife and four children, aged seven to seventeen, were given fifteen minutes to take one bed and some of their clothes before they burned the house.

In October, Steele was arrested at his farm again—this time by Captain James Kincheloe and one other man—and taken to Fredericksburg on his own horse. He was told he would be released if he took the Confederate oath of allegiance. Refusing, he stayed in prison until March 1863, when he was turned over to the United States government at City Point.

On December 28, Major General J.E.B. Stuart made a raid on Burke Station along the Orange and Alexandria Railroad. It was during this raid that Stuart boldly complained to the U.S. government that the mules he captured were of poor quality.[205]

Civilian William Holsapple of Burke Station lived close enough to go down to the station to see what was going on during the raid and ended up face to face with the famous Confederate himself. He "saw a bright fire at the station and [with] two sutlers went down to ascertain the cause of the fire. [They] walked right into the Rebel Lines and were taken prisoners by the Rebels. [Holsapple] was brought before General Stuart and General Fitzhugh Lee. These officers wished to know who he was and if he was a spy." Local residents came forward and "said they were well acquainted" with Holsapple. They stated, "He was a quiet and peaceable man. General Stuart then commanded [Holsapple] to stand upon the Rail Road track and not to move until they [the Rebels] were out of sight, and then that he could return home and [go] about his own business."

Free of the Confederates, Holsapple returned home only to find Union soldiers at his house. Telling Major Rogers (of the 123rd Regiment of the New York Volunteers) where he had just been and whom he had just seen, Holsapple then instructed the major to go upstairs and take his uniform off and hide in his bed. Holsapple hid the major's uniform and put his own clothing out next to the bed. Holsapple then went back downstairs and told all the sutlers in the area to hide so they would not be taken prisoner by the nearby Confederates. Stuart did not return, however, and neither prisoners nor army supplies were taken.[206]

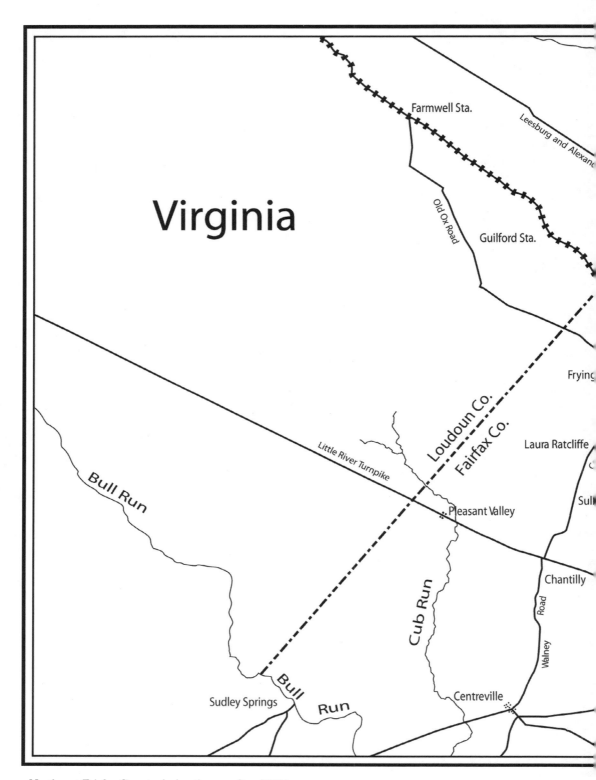

Virginia

Farmwell Sta.

Leesburg and Alexan

Old Ox Road

Guilford Sta.

Frying

Loudoun Co.

Fairfax Co.

Laura Ratcliffe

Little River Turnpike

Bull Run

Sul

Pleasant Valley

Chantilly

Cub Run

Road

Walney

Bull

Run

Sudley Springs

Centreville

Northwest Fairfax County during the war. *Steve Wolfsberger.*

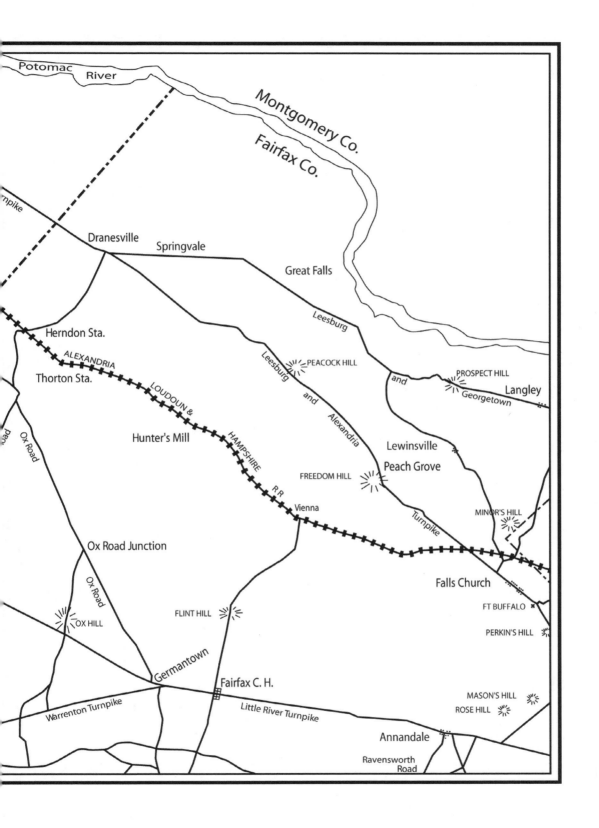

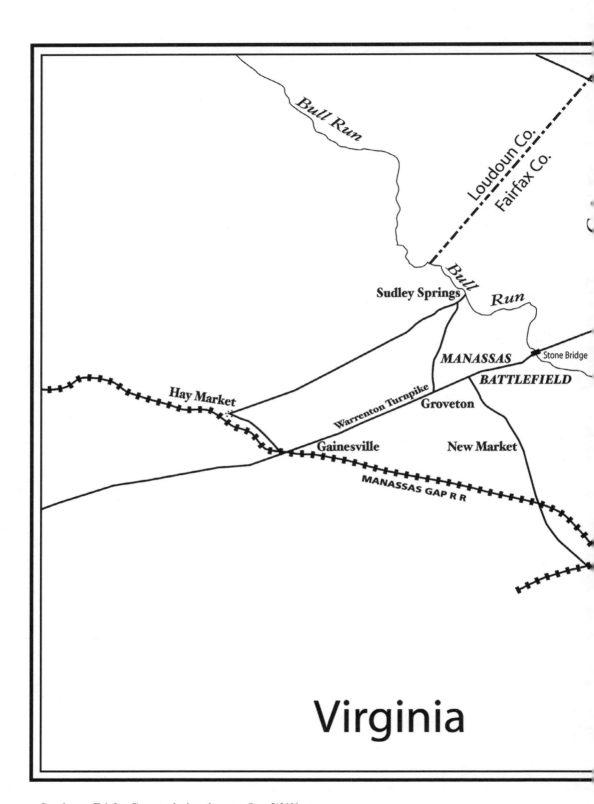

Southwest Fairfax County during the war. *Steve Wolfsberger.*

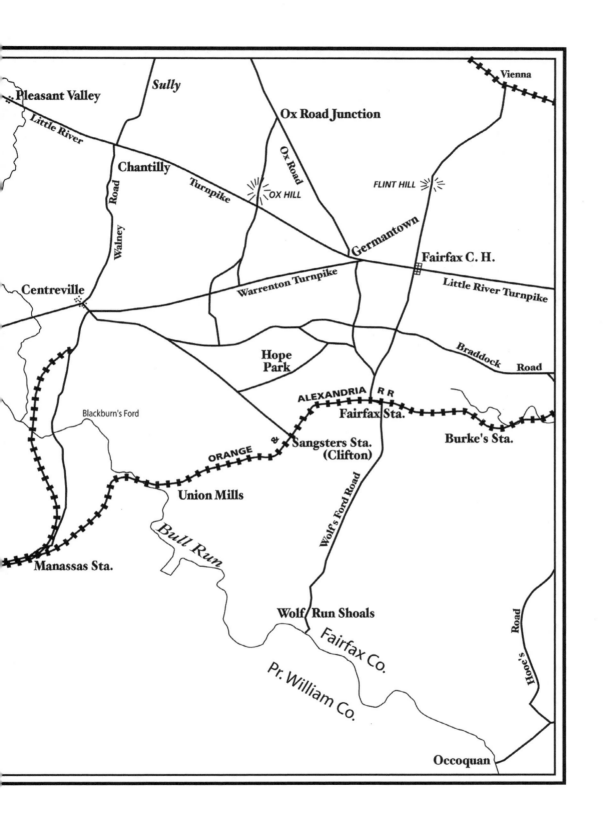

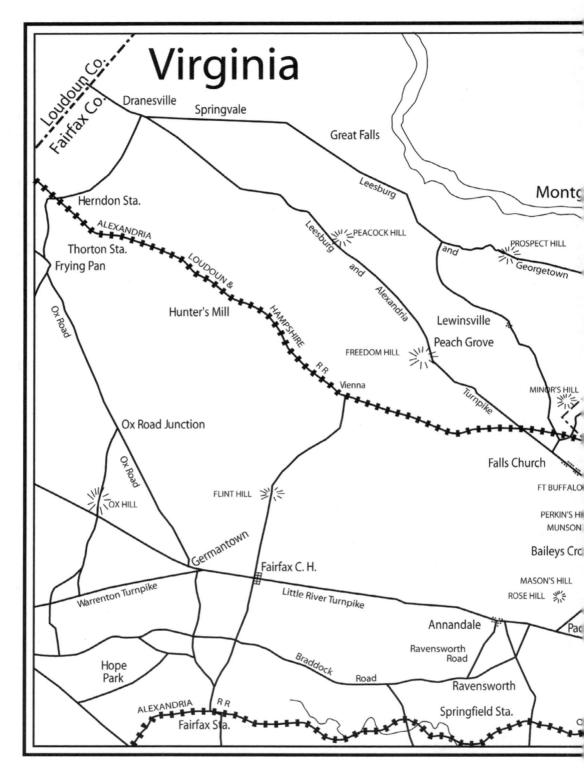

Northeast Fairfax County during the war. *Steve Wolfsberger.*

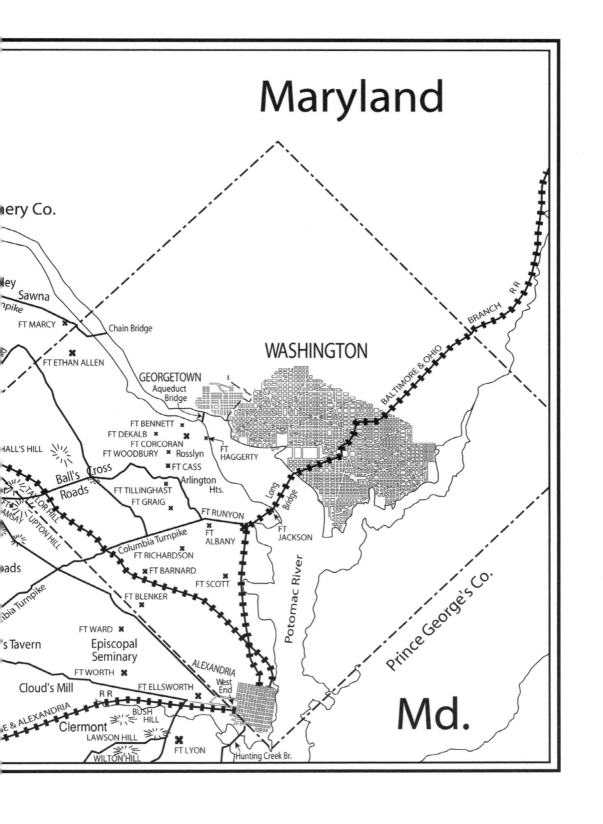

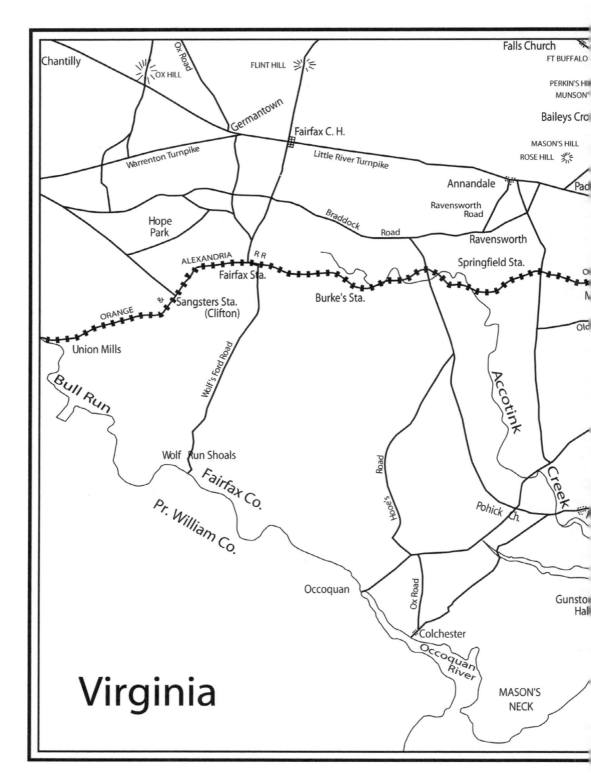

Southeast Fairfax County during the war. *Steve Wolfsberger.*

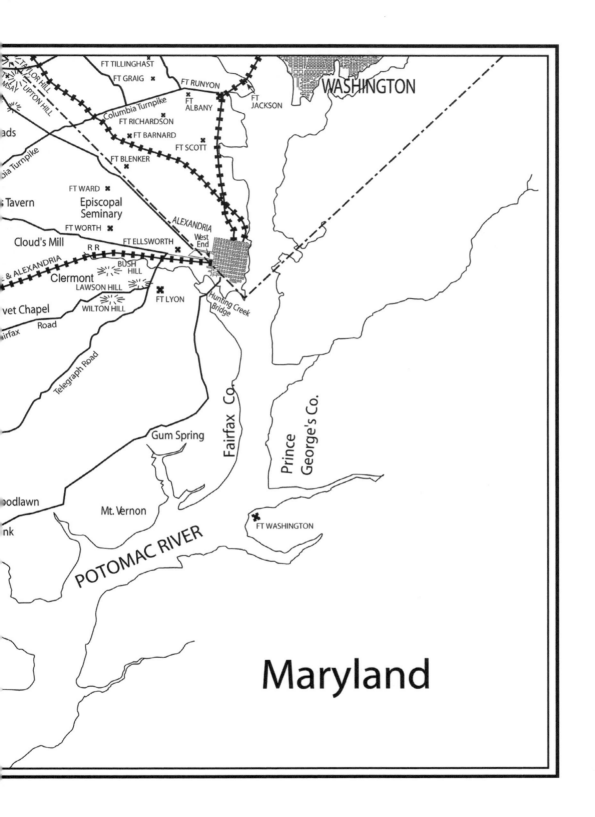

FT TILLINGHAST
FT GRAIG
FT RUNYON
WASHINGTON

TAYLOR HILL
MSAY
UPTON HILL
FT ALBANY
FT JACKSON

Columbia Turnpike
FT RICHARDSON
FT BARNARD
FT SCOTT

bia Turnpike
FT BLENKER

ads

Tavern
FT WARD

Episcopal
Seminary
FT WORTH

Cloud's Mill
R R
FT ELLSWORTH

ALEXANDRIA
West
End

& ALEXANDRIA
Clermont
BUSH
HILL
LAWSON HILL

vet Chapel
WILTON HILL
FT LYON

Hunting Creek
Bridge

airfax
Road

Telegraph Road

Gum Spring

Fairfax Co.

Prince George's Co.

odlawn
Mt. Vernon

nk
FT WASHINGTON

POTOMAC RIVER

Maryland

GUERILLA WARFARE

Military operations in Fairfax County for the next two years of the war, 1863 and 1864, can best be described as guerilla warfare—hit and run ambushes by the Confederates against the supply and communication lines of the Federal forces in control of Northern Virginia. This method presented a radical departure from the accepted form of warfare between organized armies on a defined battlefield.

The most successful and visible Confederate group to participate in these tactics in Northern Virginia was the Forty-third Virginia Partisan Rangers under John Singleton Mosby. Mosby's raids in Virginia around the Union capital intimidated and embarrassed the occupying Union forces. The area in Northern Virginia known as Mosby's Confederacy consisted of Fauquier, Loudoun, Prince William and Fairfax Counties. The proximity to Washington provided extensive coverage for his exploits from the nearby abundance of news corps.

Despite orders from the highest ranks of the Union army to capture Mosby and his men and "hang them without trial,"[207] Mosby would elude his pursuers throughout the end of the war. Although Mosby's targets were primarily military, he often captured or threatened civilians suspected of providing information about him to Union forces.

Although the civilians who appealed to the Southern Claims Commission would never admit to helping Mosby or any Confederate soldiers or officers, author Robert Morgan Moxham claims Mosby couldn't have succeeded solely on his own: "That the civilian population of northern Virginia was deeply involved in their [Mosby's] operations is beyond question."[208]

Laura Ratcliffe. *Herndon Historical Society.*

One Confederate veteran, Alexander Hunter, states it was not only civilians that helped Mosby in his many exploits, but that these civilians were also mainly women. "It is not too much to say of the great fame enjoyed by Mosby was won by the aid of the women of the Debatable Land [Mosby's Confederacy]; and not only by the brilliant partisan leader, and every officer under him, owed his life and erstwhile liberty to those maids and matrons. Many of Mosby's dashing and successful raids were but the outcome of information furnished by these fair dames."[209] The area of Northern Virginia was termed "debatable" as it was not completely under the control of either army during the war.

One such woman—who Mosby himself attributed to saving his life in his memoirs—was a Confederate supporter and spy named Laura Ratcliffe, who lived in Frying Pan just south of Herndon.

Laura did indeed save Mosby's life by warning him of a trap set for him near Frying Pan Church. On February 11, 1863, Mosby had met a number of his men and started toward Fairfax County. At the same time, a large number of Union troops under Lieutenant Arthur S. Palmer, Company C, First West Virginia Cavalry, were hiding in a grove of pine trees near the Frying Pan Church on Centreville Road, while a small number of men were picketing at a crossroads nearby. The Union plan was to entice Mosby to attack the small number of pickets, and then the bulk of the soldiers would rush from their hiding place to capture Mosby and his men.[210]

Laura was well known to the local Union troops as a Confederate sympathizer and friend of Mosby. Captain William Glazier, Second New York Cavalry, described her as "a very active and cunning rebel, who is known to our men, and is at least suspected of assisting Mosby not a little in his movement." Glazier noted that they took extreme precautions to keep the locations of the pickets a secret, yet, "by the means of Miss Ratcliffe and her rebellious sisterhood, Mosby is generally informed."[211]

Unfortunately for the plan, a young Union soldier came to Laura's house to buy milk and eggs and, trying to impress the attractive Southern girl, boasted openly about the trap. "We'll get Mosby this time. On his next raid he will certainly come to Frying Pan and it will not be possible for him to escape." He even told Laura he knew she would warn Mosby if she could. "I know you would give Mosby any information in your possession; but as you have no horses and the mud is too deep for women folks to walk, you can't tell him; so the time you hear of your 'pal' he will be either dead or a prisoner!"[212]

As soon as the soldier was gone with his milk and eggs, Laura set out with her sister—despite the mud—to warn local sympathizers to watch for Mosby. She walked north on Centreville Road to the home of another Confederate sympathizer named George Coleman, hoping that he would help her.[213] While at his house, she saw cavalry through a window and went out with her sister to see who they were. As the riders approached, she was at first alarmed that they may be Union soldiers, as she saw blue uniforms. She then recognized the lead rider as John Underwood, a fellow resident of Frying Pan, followed by Mosby. It turned out that Mosby's men were wearing captured Union clothing.[214]

Laura and her sister had literally come in the nick of time. The Union plan was working. Mosby had already seen the pickets and was preparing to attack. Warned by Laura and her sister of the trap, Mosby changed his plans and rode safely back to Middleburg.[215]

Mosby himself recalled the incident in his war reminiscences:

> *We then proceeded on toward Frying Pan where I heard that a cavalry picket was stationed and waiting for me to come after them. I did not want them to be disappointed in their desire to visit Richmond. When I got within a mile of it and had stopped for a few minutes to make my disposition for attack, I observed two ladies walking rapidly toward me. One was Miss Laura Ratcliffe, a young lady to whom Stuart had introduced me a few weeks before, when returning from his raid on Dumfries—with her sister. Their home was near Fryingpan, and they had got information of a plan to capture me, and were just going to the house of a citizen to get him to put me on my guard, where fortune brought them across my path. But for meeting them, my life as a partisan would have closed that day. There was a cavalry post in sight at Fryingpan, but near there, in the pines, a large body of cavalry had been concealed. It was expected that I would attack the picket, but that my momentary triumph would be like the fabled Dead Sea's fruit—ashes to the taste—as the party in the pines would pounce from their hiding-place upon me. This was not the only time during the war when I owed my escape from danger to the tact of a Southern woman.[216]*

Laura not only provided vital information to the Confederates; she also allowed her house to be used as a secret meeting place for J.E.B. Stuart, Mosby and members of his Partisan Rangers, Fitzhugh Lee and members of the Black Horse Cavalry and other notable Confederate soldiers. Laura kept an album in her house, hidden from the Union pickets, given to her by J.E.B. Stuart, in which he wrote her four poems, two original. In addition to these poems, there were a number of pages signed by her Confederate guests. Laura cleverly drew "calling cards" on the pages in pencil in the album for her guests to sign their names.

One page contains six signatures, including John S. Mosby, Major CSA; "Your friend" J.E.B. Stuart; Captain William Downs Farley, Stuart's chief scout; Sam Hardin Hairston, a major and quartermaster in Stuart's cavalry brigade; J.S.W. Hairston, a major and assistant adjutant general in Stuart's cavalry division; and William H.P. Berkeley of Alexandria, most likely a pro-Southern civilian. Since the signatures are not dated, it is impossible to know if the page was signed on the same day. Sam Hairston had been promoted to major in either June or July 1862 and Mosby was promoted to major in April 1863. Farley was killed at the Battle of Brandy Station on June 9, 1863. Mosby, Farley and Stuart and his men were at Second Manassas, and Stuart's men passed by Laura's house on September 1, 1862, the day of the Battle of Chantilly. It is possible that Stuart and his men signed the page together in the latter half of 1862 and Mosby signed the page in 1863 or later. All of the signatures are in

Signatures of J.E.B. Stuart, John S. Mosby, William Farley, Sam Hairston, J.S.W. Hairston and William Berkeley in Laura Ratcliffe's album. *Lewis Leigh Jr.*

ink except for William Berkeley, who wrote in pencil, indicating he could have also signed the page at a different time.

Among the military pages signed in her album, Laura had two pages of civilian signatures. One was of all local women. On Laura's "calling cards," this page included the signatures of Kate Coleman of Leesburg; Lucy E. Cockerille, a well-known family name in the area; Mollie Millan of "The Hermitage"; and Laura Monroe of Fairfax Court House. The house known as The Hermitage was at the intersection of the Little River Turnpike and Walney Road, just south of Laura's house and was used as a Confederate hospital after the Battle of Ox Hill. It was also used frequently by Mosby during his raids as a partisan ranger during the last two years of the war.[217] Very likely, these signatures belonged to the members of Laura's "rebellious sisterhood."

As a result of such civilian support, passes were required to be renewed by the military governor in order to keep civilians suspected of aiding the guerillas from entering

Signatures of Kate Coleman, Lucy Cockerille, Mollie Millan and Laura Monroe in Laura Ratcliffe's album. *Lewis Leigh Jr.*

Alexandria in early 1863. Passes were only awarded to those civilians who had positively established their loyalty to the Union. Permits were more closely examined than they had been in previous years, and those who held altered permits or carried family passes were refused entry.[218]

In addition to the circle of fifty-six forts and batteries surrounding Washington in the eastern part of the county, forward positions of Union lookouts were now posted in the western portion of the county at Centreville, Fairfax Court House, Fairfax Station, Union Mills, Wolf Run Shoals, Chantilly and Dranesville. It was these positions in more vulnerable areas that bore the brunt of the guerilla warfare.[219]

Despite all these precautions, Mosby made one of his most successful and highly publicized raids of the entire war. Early on the morning of March 9, Mosby, with thirty of his men, captured the sleeping Brigadier General Edwin H. Stoughton at the residence of Dr. William Presley Gunnell located near Fairfax Court House. Awaking the Brigadier General, Mosby asked, "General, did you ever hear of Mosby?" When the general responded, "Yes, have you caught him?" Mosby replied, "No, but he has caught you." Mosby and his men escaped safely passing through the Union lines at Centreville. The only resistance Mosby encountered was the wife of the post commander, who slightly delayed Mosby's men as they searched the commander's house before making their getaway.[220]

Looking for a scapegoat for the loss of a general, a letter was printed in the *New York Times* within a week, stating that "there is a woman in the town [Fairfax] by the name of Ford, not married, who has been of great service to Gen. Stuart in giving information, so much that Stuart has conferred on her the rank of major in the rebel army."[221]

Antonia Ford was indeed the daughter of a prosperous merchant in Fairfax Court House. Stuart had made Miss Ford an honorary lieutenant and aide-de-camp on his staff in October 1861 when the Confederates were in possession of the Fairfax Court House area. Following the heightened suspicion of Miss Ford, a Federal detective sent a female spy to Antonia and her father's house. She gained Antonia's trust and when Antonia showed the spy her commission from Stuart, government authorities arrested both Antonia and her father on March 13. They were first taken to Centreville before being transferred to the Old Capitol Prison in Washington under the escort of Major Joe Willard.[222]

Interestingly both of these Southern loyalists married Northerners—a destitute Miss Ratcliffe after the war to Milton Hanna and Antonia to her escort Joe Willard before the war was even over.

On March 17, Chalky Gillingham reported that the Friends Meetinghouse was used as a hospital as guerillas in citizens' dress attacked Union pickets near the Occoquan.[223]

On the same day, St. Patrick's Day, Mosby made a raid on a Union outpost at the Herndon Station on the Alexandria, Loudoun and Hampshire Railroad. This raid also involved a very frightened resident of the village of Herndon. A Union outpost had been deployed at the Herndon Train Depot. From this location, assignments were made for picket guard at Herndon Station consisting of twenty-five men under Lieutenant Alexander G. Watson, Company L, of the First Vermont Cavalry.[224]

Kitty Kitchen circa 1906. *Herndon Historical Society.*

Mosby rode toward the station with forty men. As they approached Herndon, they rode out of the woods and came upon men of the First Vermont Cavalry. Lieutenant Watson was in command of his twenty-five men from Vermont, who were resting around the old sawmill at noon with their horses tied to a nearby fence. Watson's men saw Mosby coming, but having been on picket duty for forty-eight hours, were anticipating a relief party. Mosby's men were again wearing blue overcoats, which confirmed the Union soldiers' belief. They did not realize their mistake until Mosby's men charged and quickly captured most of them, a small number rushing to the upper floor of the sawmill without having time to mount their horses.[225]

Mosby's men surrounded the sawmill, giving the Vermont men the option of surrendering or being burned alive by setting the mill on fire. As the mill was full of dry wood shavings, the men elected to surrender. One man from Vermont was shot and seriously wounded.[226] So, without firing a shot, the Union troops threw down their weapons and walked out.

As the Confederates were leaving the sawmill, they noticed four horses tied in front of Union sympathizer Nat Hanna's residence. These horses belonged to Major Wells, Captain Schofield, Lieutenant Cheney and Lieutenant Watson of the First Vermont. Wells, Schofield and Cheney had ridden to Herndon Station earlier that day to investigate charges that the pickets had been stealing from the local citizens. The four had been inside eating a meal provided by Kitty Kitchen, Hanna's wife, when they noticed the Southerners in front of the Hanna residence. Cheney and Watson rushed out, only to be captured. Wells and Schofield tried to hide in the attic. A ranger fired a shot through the ceiling calling for their surrender, causing Major Wells to fall through the attic floor into the hands of their captors below. After the war, Wells and Schofield returned to reclaim their guns, which they had hidden in the walls.[227]

Mosby recalled the incident at the Hanna house after the surrender of the men at the mill.

On going out and remounting, I observed four finely caparisoned horses standing in front of the house of Nat Hanna, a Union man. I knew that the horses must have riders, and that from their equipments they must be officers. I ordered some of the men to go into the house and bring them out. They found a table spread with milk, honey, and all sorts of nice delicacies for a lunch. But no soldiers could be seen, and Mrs. Hanna was too good a Union woman to betray them. Some of the men went upstairs, but by the dim light could see nothing on the floor. [James] Ames opened the door to the garret; he peeped in and called, but it was pitch dark, and no one answered. He thought it would do no harm to fire a shot into the darkness. It had a magical effect. There was a stir and a crash, and instantly a human being was seen descending through the ceiling. He fell on the floor right among the men. The flash of the pistol in his face had caused him to change position, and in doing so he had stepped on the lathing and fallen through. His descent had been easy and without injury to his person. He was thickly covered with lime dust and mortar. After he brushed off, we discovered that we had a major. His three companions in the dark hole were a captain and two lieutenants, who came out through the trap door, and rather enjoyed the laugh we had on the major. As we left the house the lunch disappeared with us. It was put there to be eaten.[228]

Kitty Kitchen, however, recounted the story of what happened inside the house while serving pies to her guests after her brother-in-law informed her earlier in the day that she was having the officers for dinner.

Never shall I forget that St. Patrick's Day, March 17, 1863, or them pies. As I turned from servin' the pies, I cast my eyes out'n the window, an' I saw comin' a squad of grays! The rebel yell was no louder than my scream, "the Southerns!" as they came tearin' down the hill, an' everyman at the table ran to [the] front door, the wor's thing to do, to show theyselves!, an' then the bullets jes' rained on our house. The Yankees ran inside an' I thought they was goin' to fight it out, but they buckled on sabres, they follow my brother-in-law up the stairway, till I cried out in terror.

"Gentlemen, go outside, or I'll be murdered in my own house!" Watson couldn't stand that, so he rushed out, firin' all the time, an so did Lieutenant Chiny; an I never saw either one on'em again, but I knew they'd been caught. Watson was a Vermonter, who was never more seen in these parts. The other two officers followed my brother-in-law to the garret [attic], which was floored all over an' had a big brick chimney runnin' through the roof; an' behin' that chimney was a dark cuddy protected by a closet on one side, with only three boards for floorin'. The three men crawled in there, an' while they was hidin', Mother an' me ran over to Betsy Allen's.

I looked down toward [the] mill an' saw the line of boys in blue standin' with their sabres up, an' I felt sure they would all be kilt, so I turned my back not to see it, leavin' those men hidin' in the attic. We could hear the Southerns rush in the house shootin' and bangin', an' I felt certain no one would be lef' alive. What did happen, my brother-in-law told me afterwards. Mosby's men rushed upstairs callin' them to surrender, which as the bullets whizzed 'round, they decided to do, an' they was taken prisoners of war. Nat's [her husband's] brother was lef' there, he not bein' in army, an' also known to Mosby's men, who took of with the Yankee officers an' the beautiful horses. I went creepin' home, expectin' to see dead men at every step, but I found none.

A few weeks later, Mosby's men rode by again, stopping at the Herndon Train Depot across the street from Kitty's house:

but the leader rode into our yard an' lef' his horse standin' an' knocked at the front door. "Madam," he says, "I come to apologize to you for my men shootin' at your house a week or do back." "So they did," I replied, but said no more. "Can you let me have a newspaper to read, Madam?" (There was a pile inside) but I answered, "No, sir, I can't." Mosby was too polite to insist, an' he turned an' walked away. I never saw him after, but in his book he called me a "Union woman"; he little knew how my heart was torn to pieces. I grew nervous seein' scouts at all hours, an' soldiers rushin' by with bayonets pointed at my home. But let that pass, an' bygones be bygones.[229]

Life was getting more difficult for the civilians living in the county, suffering from both lack of food and disease. In April, Anne Frobel recounted in her diary that all her provisions were "entirely exhausted, not an ear of corn, or a grain of any kind on the place, and none to be had in the neighborhood that we know of. The supply at the mills is very scant, and prices enormous. Later in the day [a neighbor] brought us a small loud [*sic*] of hay and cheering news. His family of seven are just recovering from the small pox."[230]

Skirmishing continued throughout the county as major battles continued elsewhere during the year; Fairfax was spared any further major battles. Union soldiers marched from point to point on reconnaissance and scouting expeditions. Because of the fear of J.E.B. Stuart and Mosby, Union soldiers were on constant alert. In order to continue building fortifications, Major John Barnard, in charge of the Union defenses, hired one thousand colored men to build further defenses in Alexandria. Soldiers escorted all the unemployed blacks about town wherever work was needed, excavating areas where stockades, barricades and bastions were then built.[231]

William Holland of Accotink was born a free man and had forty cords of wood taken in February 1863 as Union troops were headed to the Battle of Chancellorsville: "There was a couple of pickets near where the wood was and they set the fires and burn it up." Holland was described as a "smart, intelligent black man. His mother belonged to General Washington."[232]

In May, a squad of cavalry passed by John F. Webb's place in Falls Church. "On their return [his] horses disappeared."[233]

James Coleman complained about cabbage being taken from his farm in Vienna in May through July the same year. "Troops were keeping garrison at Fort Lyon, Fort Ellsworth and Fort Ward. They even came down from Fort Worth. I would go to the fort to see about it and they would not allow me to go in. They would come at night and get it."[234]

On June 2, an explosion at Fort Lyon, one and a half miles from Alexandria, shattered windows and cracked plaster in the town. While working on a magazine, a shell was accidentally detonated, killing twenty-three soldiers. Anne Frobel recorded the event in her diary the same day: "About two oclock today we were startled by a most violent thundering explosion, followed by another, in quick succession, the earth shook and trembled. I was so frightened, I thought I saw the logs tumbling out and falling all about. I looked up at Ft Lyon which presented a splendid appearance, just like my idea of a large volcano. We were too far off to see or hear any thing more." A curious servant ventured over to the fort and came back horrified at what she saw: "She says a great number were killed, and many more wounded, she never beheld such a sight, the men dragging out the crushed, mangled bodies from the dirt and rubbish, some without heads, the dismembered bodies, and dissevered limbs are scattered all around the fort and through the woods and fields in every direction."[235]

A typical story during the war. The home of Mrs. Wilcoxson near Camp Wolf Run Shoals where Lieutenant Carmi L. Marsh, Thirteenth Regiment of the Vermont Volunteers, was sick and taken care of in January and February of 1862. *Fairfax County Public Library, Photographic Archives.*

By June, Anne had only two cows left to provide milk. One of her neighbors took the cream from the milk to buy necessities for her sister, Anne, and servants. Neighbors also brought her tea while neighborhood children hunted birds and rabbits for them for food.[236]

Chalky Gillingham reported the reduction of Union forces in his area as they marched to Gettysburg, causing him "great alarm. Small Guerilla bands [were] roving about, stealing horses and colored men. They took three colts out of our pasture, and four horses and several men from Woodlawn Mansion."[237]

County civilians continued to suffer at the hands of the Union armies even as Union soldiers left the county. Sanford W. Cooksey in Centreville complained about General Hooker taking supplies on his way to Gettysburg. Timber, fence, corn and oats were taken from Uriah Ferguson at Fairfax Court House throughout the year. Troops near Dranesville took the materials of Charles W. Kitchen's house, outbuildings, lumber and brick near Herndon to construct their barracks during the winter.[238]

Benjamin Lewis and his wife lived at Fairfax Court House and had been free for two or three years before the war. When asked how he came to own property, he replied, "I worked, and I had cows and a wagon. I worked for a man and gardened for him, marketed for him and did what he wanted, and he paid me $25 a month, and I boarded myself." Lewis had one daughter and rented thirty acres. He "raised fruit and garden crops, had a young hired boy. I was for the Union; I wasn't for no disturbance at any time." He had property taken in 1863.

His daughter, Caroline Smith, provided testimony about Union soldiers taking cows and pigs, although she unable or unwilling to confirm her relationship to her father. When she was asked about being the daughter of Mr. Lewis, she replied, "I don't know; some people says I am. My mother says so." She claimed the Dutch—"Garibaldis"—of General Blenker's division were camped between Fairfax Court House and Alexandria. They also took her flour and meal. "Two of them came in and said they wanted a Johnny Cake, and I said I Hadn't nothing, and one of them turned around and looks back in the closet and said 'here is planty for 2 or 3 Johnny cakes'; and others came in, and they rolled it out and said that they would pay for it, that they were short of rations."[239]

Robert T. Scisson of Fairfax Station claimed $25 for a wagon used to carry the wounded and sick that was never returned, and $100 for one hundred bushels of corn taken in 1863. Though a typical claim for loss of property, Scisson did have depositions from three Union soldiers for whom he had provided care at Scisson's home while General Mead's army fell back from Culpeper.[240]

Fairfax, October 20, 1863
This is to certify that I have staid with Mr. Scisson 2 days and he is a good Union man, in every way doing all he can to please the troops of the Union. He is not with the Confederates.
Joseph Smith
George W. Heath
2nd Mass. Vols. U.S. 5th Corps

Fairfax Station, Oct. 20, 1863
This is to certify that I was sick and that Mr. Scisson took me into his house & treated me
kindly and him and his family did every thing that they could for me and while stopping
with him he never turned the solder away without giving him something to eat & he is I
think a good Union man & him & his family deserve the respect of the Union troops.
Johnson Melch
Co. I, 4th o.v.d, 2nd Army Corps

Union officers often took possession of property abandoned by known Confederates. Colonel Elias M. Greene, the chief quartermaster of the department of Washington, took possession of Confederate Dr. McVeigh's property near Vienna in 1863 to confiscate the hay that was growing there. Greene sent a scout to McVeigh's place, who reported a loyal Union civilian, Mason Shipman, had grown a crop of hay there under an agreement with McVeigh. The scout told Shipman that the "Col. was a rough man, and he said it didn't make a damned bit of difference." Greene ordered the scout to keep an eye on the place to keep it from being molested, as it now belonged to the government. The scout reported this to Shipman, telling him that the government was going to take the property. Shipman complained that this was wrong, as he was a Union man and paying rent to McVeigh for the place.

Shipman continued to cut the grass. The scout reported this to Greene, who sent the scout back to take the hay. Although Shipman was plenty angry about the situation, the scout told him it was of no use because "if he [Shipman] didn't give it to me [the scout], there were plenty of men at Fort Ethan Allen who would help take it if necessary." Greene then sent trains out to McVeigh's place and took and loaded all the hay that Shipman had cut and cut and loaded the rest of the field as well. The scout reported that this was done quickly in order not to attract too much attention. "We wanted to load up and get away quietly because those were bilious times. Sometimes a man would be riding around there in peace, and the next moment there would be a bullet whistling about his head."[241]

Anne Frobel described the winter of 1863 as lonely and dreary with little annoyance from the soldiers. She daydreamed of someone being kind enough to drive a wagon full of food to her door. She only survived as neighbors did occasionally stop by with food such as crackers, "a great can of oysters, packages of sugar, fruit, oranges, [and] cake." Again the neighborhood boys helped by chopping wood to keep the fires and hot water going.[242]

Attacks on Washington, Falls Church and Annandale

The last half of 1863 until the spring of 1864 was considered a quiet period around Washington. Duty by the Army of the Potomac was considered "soft" for the forty thousand troops in and around the city. By 1864, relations between the soldiers and civilians "were generally predicated less of overt hostility than upon the encroachments of Federal troops on personal property and daily lives." In the spring of 1864, the department of Washington was surprised to learn that the local farmers were not planting gardens and cultivating their farms as usual, due to their now-seasoned expectations that the soldiers would continue to take their crops and fences whenever they wanted.[243]

The alertness of the Union soldiers around Washington began to increase by the middle of the year as Mosby became more active. The bulk of the Confederate army, however, was located in the Richmond-Petersburg area, although Jubal Early's Army of the Valley was having success moving through the Shenandoah Valley. He followed this with a successful fight along the Monocacy in Maryland in July, signaling his attempt to attack the nation's capital and causing a crisis both in Baltimore and Washington.[244]

Union troops were moving north of Washington from the Southern forts as Early's troops were moving through Gaithersburg and Rockville. Early reached the outskirts of Washington on July 11 at Fort Stevens, but his eleven to twelve thousand troops did not have the strength to attack, due to the heat and hard march to reach the city. Union troops were marching just as hard through Washington to reach Fort Stevens, named after General Isaac I. Stevens, who had been killed at Chantilly the previous year. Early's inability to attack when he had the opportunity led only to skirmishing for the rest of the day.[245]

The next day, Early realized the fort had now been too strongly reinforced to attack, so he kept his skirmishes active while planning to withdraw during the night. Confederate sharpshooters made life difficult for the Union defenders. The Union forces also had to attend to the growing number of civilian spectators who had come to witness the activities, including none other than President Lincoln and his wife, Mary. Lincoln, wanting to assess the situation himself, mounted a parapet to view the Confederates before being "ordered" to move to a safer location.[246]

Early withdrew as planned that night into the morning of July 13, moved into camp in Leesburg and the biggest direct threat to Washington during the war was over. The threat was not completely erased, as Confederates maintained a force in the Shenandoah Valley and Mosby's men "roved unchecked in northern Virginia." Union Major General Philip Sheridan was dispatched to eliminate Early from the valley in August, and it would take until the following spring to succeed after victories at Winchester, Fisher's Hill, Cedar Creek and Waynesboro. Mosby, however, would never be defeated, caught or killed in his continuing effort to harass Sheridan's men and keep thousands of Union troops tied down to garrison duty around Washington.[247]

In February, Federal authorities started to sell the properties of civilian refugees, some Confederate, who were delinquent in paying their taxes. Over two hundred properties were sold and in one day in Alexandria the Union authorities raised $24,795.[248]

Chalky Gillingham reported the high level of Rebel activity in his area in his journal in February: "I do not wish to describe all the incidents and scenes of the Rebellion now raging around us, it would fill many volumes. Suffice it to say that wandering parties infest the country all around, acting the part of Robbers, Highwaymen and Horse thieves. They are kept out of our settlement by the inhabitants arming themselves and keeping watch day and night."[249]

General J.E.B. Stuart reported in February that Mosby kept "a large force of the enemy's cavalry continually employed in Fairfax in the vain effort to suppress his inroads." Mosby routed a California regiment in Dranesville on February 22. In July, guerilla bands "infested" Falls Church and the areas west. An additional eight hundred Union troops were posted in Falls Church to combat the guerilla activity that, correctly or incorrectly, was always attributed to Mosby. Troops were sent from Falls Church to capture Mosby, and the Federals were routed along the Little River Turnpike in Aldie.[250]

In August, sixty-nine men from Falls Church were routed by forty to fifty of Mosby's men on Braddock Road near Falls Church and at Fairfax Station. Mosby fearlessly repaid this attention by raiding Falls Church on August 24, 25, 31 and twice on September 1. On August 24 he kidnapped a Northern sympathizer before releasing him to take a message to the Federal authorities that he had captured two Union officers in retaliation for two of Mosby's men being sentenced to prison. On the twenty-fifth, he stole two soldiers and four horses. On September 13, Mosby crept into the Thirteenth New York's camp at night, managing to capture the brigade butcher.[251]

Mosby did not spare the Union troops in Annandale. On August 11, 1863, Mosby and his men captured two Union wagon trains and all the accompanying horses and mules, as well as twenty-five prisoners. Attempting to follow up that success, Mosby tried to make off with a herd of horses on August 25, and although Mosby was wounded in his side and thigh in the fight, his men carried the day. Carrying the wounded Mosby in a wagon, the rangers escaped toward Aldie with twelve prisoners and the horses. Mosby's wounding led to rumors of his demise, but after a month of recuperation, he was able to rejoin his command.[252]

A year later, Mosby returned. After his previous hit-and-run attacks, Mosby set his sights on a 170-man detachment at a stockade that guarded Annandale (probably located at the present-day intersection of the Little River Turnpike and Hummer Road). On the morning of August 25, pickets at the stockade fired upon Mosby's men. In return, Mosby had two pieces of artillery open fire on the stockade. The Union troops barely had enough time to wake up and stop a charge of one hundred Rebels against the stockade entrance. Mosby then sent a demand for a Union surrender.

When the Union soldiers refused, Mosby continued a somewhat ineffective bombardment. Sending a later demand for the stockade's surrender, Union Captain Mickles told the second Confederate messenger bearing a white handkerchief, "Tell Colonel Mosby I will not surrender, and if he sends that rag up here again I'll shoot it to hell." After a few more shots, Mosby withdrew, with the "Battle of Annandale" becoming an unsuccessful raid in Fairfax County.[253]

These raids and skirmishes continued throughout the county for the rest of the year. However, the growing plight of the Confederacy drew the resources from Northern Virginia, and the winter of 1864–1865 was fairly quiet. Anne Frobel recorded the winter in her diary as "another miserable, wretched winter, of want and privation," as Wilton Hill was still filled with Union soldiers. She was also hearing accounts from newspaper accounts that the South was losing the war: "O wretched, wretched, people that we are, if we have always have these low inhuman, selfish, tyrants to rule over us."[254]

One of the homes in Fairfax County put up for sale in 1864 by Federal authorities was Clermont, the property of Commodore French Forrest of the Confederate navy. Located three miles west from Alexandria on the Orange and Alexandria Railroad, Clermont was put up for sale on July 19 under the Confiscation Act of 1862. Two Union officers, John Bigelow and Westel Willoughby, purchased the house for $1,900; the 198 acres was estimated to be worth $40,000 to $50,000.

The property was not delivered until September 26, 1865, as the Union army had been using the house as a hospital for smallpox victims since 1862. Upon being notified that he could finally take possession of his property, John Bigelow found that the house had inadvertently burned to the ground upon the Union army's withdrawal.

The sale took a further twist when Douglas Forrest, the son of French Forrest and a colonel in the Confederate army, filed a suit in 1867 upon the death of his father against the two new owners for recovery of his father's land. The State Courts of Virginia decided the case in Forrest's favor based on their finding that Bigelow and Willoughby had only purchased the estate for the lifetime of French Forrest. The litigation continued to the Supreme Court and in 1869 the Supreme Court affirmed that the land belonged to Douglas Forrest.

In 1871, John Bigelow applied for a payment of $100 a month to the Southern Claims Commission for the use of the Forrest property as a hospital. The commission rejected his claim stating they had no jurisdiction in rent claims. In the end, all he received for his $1,900 was "a costly and unsuccessful litigation."[255]

A colored man from Langley, William L. Ashton, made a claim for hay taken from him while living in a house that belonged to Benjamin Meakle in 1864. He had served as a cook for the Bucktail Regiment from Baltimore for nine months until he was disabled after getting his feet "frosted" during the winter. He moved to Fairfax County in 1862 and was married. He lived in one of the houses belonging to Mr. Meakle to keep it from being destroyed by the Union army. An overseer from a local Freedmen's Camp, which had grown produce for the Federal army under Major Elias M. Greene, took his hay.

James W. Green, who lived near Vienna, had ten acres of corn, a half-acre of potatoes and a four-year-old iron gray horse taken by Union soldiers under General Wright, who had stopped for the night near Green's premises in July 1864. He had a general store in Falls Church with permission for the Federal army to conduct trade. He was also arrested by Confederates during the war and made a daring escape:

> *I was arrested once by the rebels. I was taken by a squad of Mosbys men the night of the 18th of November 1863. The Union forces were in Vienna at the time, the rebels came to my house after night, and arrested me, and took me away. They started to take me away to Mosbys Head Quarters near Piedmont. When we got about two miles I made my escape. I knew when the road was narrow with the second growth of pines on each sides. I had made my mind that when we reached the place, I would jump from my horse and make my escape at the risk of my life.*
>
> *The night was pretty dark, and after they left my house, [there were] only two in charge of me. When we reached this narrow place, we discovered a large charcoal wagon and team going in the same direction, the road being narrow we had to separate, to pass the wagon. I dropped behind the one [Rebel] who took the same side of the wagon that I did. I took from my pocket a spur in my hand, and struck my horse with it, at the same time turned him around and rode back hard as my horse could go, striking my horse with the spur in my hand at every jump. One of them followed me, and fired at me three times. I did not stop until I reached Vienna and reported to our troops.*

Green believed he was arrested simply because he was a Union man. He had voted against the Ordinance of Secession.[256] Green's daughter, Virginia, gave a detailed description of all that happened during the one night the Union soldiers spent at her and her father's house and took their horse.

In the summer of 1864 the Union troops came to our place, and remained over night. I remember some of the officers had their Head Quarters at our house. I recollect the seargun [Sergeant] gave me a present of a silver pen holder and a gold pen. I remember seeing them putting their cattle in the cornfield and seeing some of the soldiers carrying of corn fodder in their arms and feeding it to their horses. I also remember seeing them digging potatoes and eating them. I saw the men cooking them around the house at their fires. They were encamped all around the house.

I remember seeing them taking the rails of fence and making their fires. I remember seeing the soldiers catching the fowls, and seeing my mother cooking them for the soldiers. The same soldiers took all there was in the garden. The horse was taken the next day after they came, she was grey, a sort of iron grey. I never saw her afterwards. [257]

FINAL REVIEW

Although the war was coming to a close in the beginning of 1865, the defenses around Washington continued to be manned and maintained at a high level. In January, there were 31,000 effective fighting men out of 37,000 men on the muster rolls, supported by close to 1,000 pieces of artillery.[258]

There were arguments on both sides of having so many men in place in case of an attack on Washington. President Lincoln was not convinced there would not be another attack on the capital city. General Ulysses S. Grant felt "there is not the slightest need for apprehension, except from a dash of a few mounted men into Alexandria, and with proper watchfulness this ought not to occur."[259]

Mosby's men continued to keep the Union troops in place, however, and the number of troops and guns around Washington actually grew through the early months of the year, as Sheridan's role in the Shenandoah was reduced. Some of the Union soldiers were needed to perform maintenance, as the dirt in the forts eroded and wood needed replacement. And even as the threat of an attack on Washington was truly winding down, General Lee was pinned down in Petersburg, and the effort to maintain the forts was kept up in part for possible attacks from future enemies.[260]

The end of the war—and with it the end of the threat to Washington—finally came as the roads dried in the spring, and the armies were able to play out the final action, ending with Lee's surrender on April 9. Closer to the capital city, Mosby disbanded his men later that month. The final flurry of activity in the defenses around the city occurred not due to a Confederate attack, but due to the assassination of President Lincoln on April 14.

The question of the dismantling of the defenses around Washington would follow shortly thereafter. Of the now seventy-four enclosed forts and armed batteries, fifty-one were to be dismantled at once, which Grant agreed to on June 19. Hiring civilians fulfilled the need for labor as the soldiers were mustered out of service after the Grand Review in Washington on May 23 and 24 and left for their old homes.[261]

As the soldiers left Fairfax County, the destruction of the county they left behind was ever more evident:

> *The scene was one of desolation from Alexandria to the Bull Run battlefield. Observers of the dedication of the monuments on that battlefield in June 1865 remembered that a "few decrepit houses and leaning chimneys" were all that remained around Fairfax Court House. The local men "with their homes ruined, their families beggared and themselves humbled" drew the sympathy of the more fortunate city dwellers from Washington. Throughout northern Virginia "fences are utterly swept away, occasionally a small patch of corn or wheat is passed, but the whole face of the country is changed. Scrub oak and pine are springing up everywhere." Centreville was a desert as late as 1914. The war had killed that village of rare beauty.[262]*

Chalky Gillingham recorded the close of the war in his diary on April 1:

> *Early in the last month the rebellion was brought to a speedy close by the capture of the Commander-in-Chief of the Rebellious forces, Robert E. Lee, and his whole army. Soon after this Jeff Davis, their pretended president, was also captured, together with most of their leading men.*
>
> *On the night of the 14th of last month the President—A. Lincoln—was assassinated by order of the leading Rebels. An attempt [was made upon] the lives of Secretary Seward and the rest of the Cabinet, which did not prove successful. The Country was thrown into utmost sorrow and mourning at this diabolical act.[263]*

Anne Frobel also wrote of the end of the war in her diary in April:

> *And then the news that Gen. Lee had surrendered. But we did not take any notice, did not put the slightest faith in the report, had learned of it so often in the past two or three years, until the morning of the 4 or 5th of April, when the simultaneous burst of cannon from all the efforts around and in Wa.*
>
> *O mercy! That was another day not to be forgotten. I neither ate nor drank. I threw myself down on my face and cried. O it was an exceedingly bitter cry. But it is useless, I cannot depict the agony of that day.*
>
> *On Saturday the 15th of April, something had gone wrong. Last night the president and all his cabinet was murdered, and I cannot tell how many others. Very little information could be obtained the wildest commotion reigned every where. Every avenue to the city was barred not a living thing was allowed to pass in or out, of either of the three places Washington, Georgetown, or Alex. The military was out on force to capture the murders.*

But after a day or two we learned the name of the murderer was Boothe, John Wilks Boothe. I think with horror of his sufferings, traveling, and hiding about for days and days with a broken leg. Poor, poor creature, none but a mad man would have ever dreamed of committing an act.

Life in Alexandria slowly started to return to normal. By mid-June the stockades were removed, easing travel. The office of military governor was discontinued on July 7, and the military surplus was auctioned during the summer. Farmers were able to buy horses, cattle, spades, shovels, shirts, drawers and blankets. The seminary hospital was closed in mid-August.[264]

The population of Alexandria had increased from four thousand from the beginning of the war to seventeen thousand. Many of the increased population were free blacks, who now almost equaled the number of white residents. A majority owned their own homes and worked for wages.[265]

Their presence was still not accepted by some of the white population, as Anne Frobel wrote: "We walked into town on Saturday last, and found the streets filled with Negroes, all rushing along in gangs and looking at all the white people in the most sullen and insolent manner. I am sure I was not run against less than six times by negro men while walking down King Street. They would take you with their baskets, and yell and whistle right in your ear. Some times it was deafning, and push you off the side walks, or run you over the cellar doors. We could scarcely walk the streets for them."[266]

James S. Purdy lived in Annandale and had a relationship with Union soldiers that began on July 22, 1861, after First Bull Run, and lasted the entire war. He claimed his property was occupied until May 1865.[267]

After the end of the war, General Sheridan's army camped on William S. Reid's farm on Franconia Road, about three and a half miles from Alexandria, for three to four weeks leading up to the Grand Review in Washington at the end of May 1865.[268]

John Dean of Springfield claimed he had hay and horses taken after the army returned from Richmond and before the Grand Review. One of the horses taken was a "splendid stallion valued at about $300."[269]

At the end of the war, John Haislip of Mason Neck had been without his means of earning a living since August of 1861. He was a part owner of a boat, *Pocahontas*, which was taken on a Sunday morning. The boat was rigged as a schooner and had a cabin, centerboard and two masts. Haislip used it to haul wood to Alexandria and Washington. By the end of the war, the boat was in ruins at Fort Washington.[270]

Mary A. Gossom of Fairfax Station claimed that General Sherman's army marched by her farm in May as well and camped there for one or two days, using 405 panels of oak and chestnut rails for fuel.[271]

Union troops, including Sheridan's cavalry, were sprawled around Falls Church from Munson's and Upton's Hills to Bailey's Cross Roads, waiting for their dismissal. Their two-month stay signaled an increase of the soldiers' foraging for food and hay and land for grazing horses, putting civilians once again directly in the path of the soldiers' needs.[272]

The heirs of Phyllis Pearson of Burke's Station claimed that seventy-four acres of wood were cut from her farm from August of 1864 up to May of 1865. "It was the best in the community and I have been told it was the oldest."[273]

After the war, John Jackson, who lived at Broad Run, recalled in his memories: "I was called free, born free, but I was not free. I said that about the time the war was going to commence; that my children, that I would like to have my children go to school and they took me and whipped me." They were "Enoc Low, Mack Low, and others. They took me to Richmond and they held me there. This was about the time of the Dranesville fight [December 1861]. I staid there until March following; then I was taken down to old Point Comfort and exchanged and sent to Baltimore and brought here. Then I went home and rented the Bicksler farm [Dranesville] again." Enoc Low was a member of the Rebel army. Despite voluminous testimony on Mr. Jackson's behalf, the claims commission decided this case was fraud.[274]

So how was it determined who was loyal to the United States during the Civil War? This was done by inquiring about the civilian's reputation, checking a man's voting records on Secession or by asking the civilian's neighbors, family members, slaves, coworkers and even soldiers he met during the war to determine his loyalty. In a deposition for Joseph H. Cockrell of Herndon, John Hauxhurst, who worked for General Hancock in Washington during the war and lived near Herndon, stated, "It was part of my duties to ascertain the loyal men in that section."[275]

Lewis Bailey, of Bailey's Cross Roads, had 895 cords of wood taken in February 1865 by Colonel Greene, the quartermaster who sent word that it was needed for the government. Bailey described his life during the war:

> When I first came here in 1840 I went to the farm at the crossroads and have resided there ever since. Did not leave the place during the war, not a night, nor did any member of my family. Several Union officers made their headquarters at my house, Gen. Stobel, etc. They were there from six weeks to two months at a time.
>
> I never owned any slaves and for twelve years previous to the war I would not employ a colored man to do a day's work for me. My wife had colored women in the house and she had two children bound out to her, but after the war commenced they were free. I had 320 acres, five miles from the end of the Long Bridge. About 150 acres were in woods. I bought it in 1840 and paid $6000 in cash for it. Bought it without having it surveyed. It was said to be the poorest farm in the county.[276]

George Brice, a slave, lived in Falls Church during the war. He claimed General Sheridan's army took twelve acres of corn in June 1865 after the fall of Richmond. "I was a Union man. Did nothing for rebels only what I was obliged to. William Y. Dulin was my master. I think he was a rebel. I came away in 1861. I went to General Blinker's [sic] headquarters near the Long Bridge and then was sent to McClellan's Headquarters. I was in the Government employ for a while and then went back. I never was near rebels during [the] war and never saw one until after the war." The heirs of William Y. Dulin made a claim that Colonel Greene cut timber from his farm southwest of Falls Church in 1864 and 1865 but did not receive an allowance.[277]

Ambrose Barcroft, who lived close to Bailey's Cross Roads after having his mill taken earlier in the war, had ten acres of grass destroyed in the spring of 1865, when Captain Prawl's cavalry came and turned their horses upon the grass.[278]

The war also caused neighbors on the same side to quarrel among each other. Joseph Sewell lived near Langley, was a Union man and voted against Secession. One of his neighbors was also a Union man, as were both of their wives. The neighbor's wife was an "excitable Union woman," who frequently left during the war to escape possible trouble with Confederates. When she and her husband left, they asked Sewell to watch over their farm. When Sewell's wife asked the neighbor's wife why she left so often, the neighbor's wife told her she "had no right to know, and a difficulty occurred between the two women. And in order to get revenge I think she caused my arrest [by Southern forces]. That is the only way I can account for it." Sewell was only held for three to four hours, but he believed he would not have been arrested if it weren't for the women's troubles with each other.[279]

Samuel Sharper was a free black man who lived at Prospect Hill near Lewinsville. He talked about his loyalty to the Union with a Mr. Edward Oliver, who was a Southerner. "Mr. Oliver seemed to be right much disturbed because I would talk in favor of the United States. Oliver said the north had more men than the south but the south was in the right and bound to whip. I said to him, 'you say the north has a great many more men than the south, perhaps it will be like a big dog jumping on a little dog.' He got very mad and said if I did not mind how I talked it would not be well for me."

Sharper also noticed a particular man frequently bringing out supplies to Washington. "The man was Montgomery King. Had two sons in the rebel army. I was determined to put a stop to it. I told James Wren and he went to the union camp and told Gen. Augur. So King did not come out any more."[280]

Two other black men told the commission how they lived and worked during the war. John Jackson gave a deposition for Archibald Merchant, who lived in Langley. Of Mr. Merchant, he said, "He is a friend of mine; always has been since I was raised. I was raised a slave and am a colored man and he is a white man, that is the only difference. I was set free by emancipation. I was free about 15 or 16 years before the war." He had "served my time with a man named James Payne."[281]

John Blackston "was made free by the war." Presumably he left his master and worked during the war. "I belonged to George Mason of Spring Bank, Fairfax County. Worked for James McWilliams during [the] war for four years. I worked for him after the fall of Richmond. The first three years I worked for him he gave me $0.75 a day and my board. The last year he gave me $0.50 a day and my board. I grubbed, ploughed, planted, hauled rails, cleaned up the land and cut wood."[282]

William Lipscomb talked about the difficulties of dealing with both Union and Confederate soldiers during the war. He lived near Munson's Hill. "We were compelled, the most of us there in the neighborhood, to stand as it were, aloof. If there was one of them came on either side, and asked for a drink of water, a glass of milk, or a piece of bread, we had to give it, and it was useless for us to refuse anything because they could come and take it and [they] did take it."[283]

Mrs. Charlotte E. Read had severe difficulties after Confederates killed her husband, John Read, in October of 1864. John was a member of the Union Home Guards, and the couple lived near Bailey's Cross Roads. One night a number of Rebels came to the Reads' house from Annandale, three miles away. They claimed to be Union troops, having come to warn the people in Falls Church of an attack from the Rebels. There were very few Union troops around the Reads' house at the time, just the Home Guards.

John Read told her, "Wife, I think they are coming. We can hear the horses hoofs; but I do not know who they are. We shall soon know, because they will have to pass the Union pickets before they get to us." The Reads heard the Union picket halt them, and there was a great deal of confusion. When the body of men came up to the gate, John Read asked who they were. They replied that they were the Eighth Illinois. Mrs. Read said that the Eighth Illinois had recently been stationed there, and her husband believed the Rebels at their gate were indeed the Eighth Illinois.

The Home Guards were made up of both white and colored men. Mrs. Read then heard one of the Rebels say, "Shoot them, Shoot every damned one of them" and heard a number of shots fired. She thought all of the Home Guards were killed and went upstairs to hide. She saw the Rebels taking her husband and another man away and hoped that her husband would get away and make it back. The next day, the only person to return was the other man the Rebels had taken. He had no boots, hat or coat and told her that "Mr. Read had been taken thirteen miles, and shot."

Mrs. Read's daughter and her aunt went out looking for her husband and found his body. "He was dead, had been shot right through his ear and neck."[284]

AFTERMATH AND
SUMMARY OF CLAIMS

Those civilians who returned to Fairfax County after the war were as depressed as the land they found waiting for them. "The scars of the war were left deep upon the breast of Fairfax County. Probably no other county suffered to an equal extent."[285]

Returning Confederates had lost the war, their loved ones and most of their property. The only solution was for farmers to work hard to attempt to cultivate whatever crops they could. Women used all their talents to refurbish what was left in order to restore their homes. "Ladies once accustomed to leisurely living prepared meals over open fires and scrubbed family laundry."[286] Everyone made an effort to reopen schools, churches and roads and to rebuild bridges and rail lines.

Despite the lack of capital, Northerners were willing to allow credit to their old customers, taking advantage of military surplus sales to purchase bargains to help them restock and restart their farms. By August, court was held at Fairfax Court House for the first time in three years. A local newspaper reporter noted the area around the courthouse was beginning to be rebuilt. "Stores are being reopened, houses repaired, and fencing replaced. The day may come when Fairfax will rise from the ruins and call upon her friends to settle within her borders."[287]

Many Union officers and soldiers also settled in the county after the war. Many had passed through and some had even fought in the area. Moving south from areas such as New York, Pennsylvania and Massachusetts to a warmer climate led them to purchase large tracts of inexpensive land.

As for the Old South, many whites longed for their old customs and ways but felt they never really wanted to leave the Union. They felt life was better for them now that the slaves were free, as some had long held concerns about slavery. Blacks were eager to expand on their newfound freedom. The influx of Northerners helped in the rapid establishment of black settlements within the county.

It is hard to represent Fairfax County as a typical cross section of the South as it was among the northernmost counties in the South. As in the case of the Barnes family at Hope Park, the cost of slaves was growing exorbitant before the war and "slavery was a declining institution in the District, Southern Maryland and Northern Virginia when the war broke."[288]

By June of 1865, only twenty-five fortifications surrounding the city of Washington were still being operated. By November, however, the cost of maintaining these defenses was deemed unnecessary by the War Department and the remaining sites were abandoned.

The Freedmen's Bureau opened office in Fairfax County in August 1865 to protect the former slaves "from oppression and imposition and encouraged them to industry and economy" and to secure "fair remuneration for faithful labor."[289] One of the bureau's first responsibilities was to determine the number of blacks by county. Fairfax had 2,941 in the fall of 1865, primarily living where they always had, on the lands of their masters where they had few problems finding work as farm laborers at $10 a month for men and $5 a month for women. By the end of the decade, sharecropping had become popular and wages increased to $12 and $6 per month, respectively. Only a few blacks were able to buy land and prosper; most were only able to survive and stave off hunger.

Most white civilians still had problems with black freedom. Most energy, however, was spent in cooperating with each other rather than in hostilities. By 1870 Fairfax County's agricultural economy had recovered substantially from the war. Schools, churches, railroads, mills, telegraph lines and post offices were rebuilt and reopened. The polarized views that existed at the end of the war evolved to a more centrist posture as the decade came to a close.

In 1867 the Reconstruction Acts were passed, turning Southern states into military districts. Voter registration began in order to choose delegates to form new state constitutions acceptable to Congress and the population in order to be readmitted into the Union. In September 1867, Major General John Schofield, of the First Military District, called for an election to be held to select delegates to draft a new constitution for Virginia. There was, however, a division between the Radical Republicans, who favored quick reentry to the Union, and the conservative Democrats, who feared the voting power of newly freed slaves.[290]

Fairfax County was allowed one delegate and one at-large delegate to the state convention. The Radical Republicans' candidate was Orrin E. Hine, a recent settler from New York. The Democrats' candidate was Mottram Dulany Ball, of the established Fairfax County family, and lieutenant colonel of the Eleventh Virginia Cavalry, CSA. Across Virginia, the Republicans gained 60 percent of the votes. Of the 105 delegates statewide, 72 were Radical Republicans and 33 Democrats. The division between the two parties was still sharp and led to a year and a half of squabbling before July 8, 1869, when the new Virginia State constitution was passed by a margin of 20 to 1.[291]

In January 1870, Virginia gained readmission to the Union. The residents of Fairfax County were once again American citizens, whites for a second time, and most blacks gaining such recognition for the first time.

Confederates returning to Annandale after the war found their property in a "deplorable state, the fences gone, the stock long since sold or driven off, and the fields already high in weeds." The former slaves were even less fortunate and, with no means to be hired to support themselves, many moved to Alexandria where some relied on the government soup kitchens for their existence.[292]

In early 1866, the Freedmen's Bureau reported on an improving state of the freedman in the county: "The Refugee and Freed people of [Fairfax] County all support themselves. There is one school at Falls Church. [A school house is being built] at Fairfax Court House. [There are] about fifty houses or shantys in most of which the col'd people are living. A great many of the col'd people have leased land and are now preparing to plant and sow their grain." Another school was established at Herndon Station by June of the same year.[293]

Falls Church recovered well after the war, due mainly to its Northerners' thrift and improved farm and management techniques. For decades after the war, however, its citizens remembered those who were Northerners and who were Southerners, and coexisting members of the two groups did not socialize with each other.

The many hills in and around Falls Church that were used by the soldiers for forts and camps that defined the landscape during the war changed over time. Development covered most of their existence while some were literally decapitated for housing and business developments such as Munson's Hill, today's Apex Drive, and Perkin's Hill, today's Seven Corners.

Blacks or freedmen lived in communities in and around Falls Church and enjoyed better than average relations as almost half of the village's Home Guard had been black. When Falls Church was incorporated as a town in 1875, there were prominent black communities in and around the town. Freedmen communities also flourished in Vienna and Merrifield.

Alexandria, although scarred, had survived the war with an increased number of residents. Many of the newcomers were freed blacks, whose numbers were almost equal to the number of white residents. Many earned wages and lived on their own. A Freedmen's Court provided hope for equality.[294]

In 1869 Chalky Gillingham reported his Quaker community was flourishing. In 1871 the Quakers had started two colored schools, one at Woodlawn and one at Gum Springs. Woodlawn had a colored teacher and Gum Springs had a white teacher, each with about forty "schollars" and with another school in the planning stages.[295]

Anne Frobel did not fare well in the years after the war. The winter of 1872–1873 had left her destitute, with little money from the tenants she had taken into her house to make ends meet. In 1874 she recorded in her diary that although she was taking in boarders, the house was so dilapidated and leaking she did not know how much longer she could manage. By the end of the year, she was afraid the house would simply fall to pieces.

Woodlawn Meeting House, 102 years after the war, circa 1968. *Fairfax County Public Library, Photographic Archives.*

The destitute nature of many in the county after the war led to their submitting claims to the Southern Claims Commission in 1871. As interesting and enlightening as the stories told before the commission about life during the war were, some statistics about the claims themselves provide valuable insight about the civilian life after the war.

There were a total of 196 claims made to the commission for lost property during the war by civilians in Fairfax County. The total value of these claims was $1,031,081. Only 7 percent of the value claimed, $68,079, was allowed by the commission. On a per claim basis, the average claim was $5,261, and the average allowance was $347.

The following table provides insight of those making claims by their gender. The interesting fact was that although women made 17 percent of the claims, the value of their claims was 62 percent of the total dollar value of all claims. This was due to the exaggerated value of their claims.

Among the women who received nothing for their exorbitant claims were Mary Jones, who claimed $9,135; Anne Frobel, who claimed $35,759; Martha Corbin Ball, who claimed $54,000; Margaret Turberville, who claimed losses of $100,607; and Anna Maria Fitzhugh, who claimed $375,000. This belief that the women often exaggerated their claims or could not provide proof of ownership of their property was borne by the commission, which only rewarded 1 percent of the total of their claims. On the other hand, the commission awarded 15 percent of the value of the men's claims.

Gender	Count	Count Percent	Value of Claims	Percent of Value of Claims	Percent of Value of Claim Allowed
Female	33	17%	$640,804	62%	1%
Male	163	83%	$390,276	38%	15%
Total	196	100%	$1,031,081	$68,079*	7%

* Total value of claims allowed

The next table indicates the number and value of claims made by race. Only 11 percent of blacks in the county made claims, as all who made claims had to own and show proof of owning their property. The value of their claims is also low, representing 3 percent of the value of all the claims made in the county. The surprising fact is that their claims were believed, no doubt due to the commissioners' beliefs in blacks' loyalty to the Union cause, receiving 12 percent of the value of their claims, double the average 6 percent allowed. Joseph, Obed and Jessie Harris claimed a total of $2,311, and received half the value of their claims, or $1,145.

Race	Count	Count Percent	Value of Claims	Percent of Value of Claims	Percent of Value of Claim Allowed
Colored	21	11%	$29,410	3%	12%
White	175	89%	$1,001,670	97%	6%
Total	196	100%	$1,031,081	$68,079*	7%

* Total value of claims allowed

The area of Fairfax County where the most claims were made was the eastern portion of the county, not coincidently where the forts and camps were located just outside Washington. In this area, 62 percent of the total claims representing 74 percent of the value of all claims were made from civilians.

Region	Count	Count Percent	Value of Claims	Percent of Value of Claims	Percent of Value of Claim Allowed
East	121	62%	$760,643	74%	7%
West	65	33%	$251,414	24%	6%
Unknown	10	5%	$19,024	2%	8%
Total	196	100%	$1,031,081	$68,079*	7%

* Total value of claims allowed

Perhaps the most surprising claim was the one made by Anne Frobel herself on March 3, 1887. The total value of her claim was $35,759, a prime example of exaggeration. Her claim covered property taken from September of 1861 to August of 1865. Her claim included the loss of wood, hay, rye, turnips, potatoes, buckwheat, horses, hogs, corn, fencing and tobacco. The claim also included $10,000 for rent charged to the Union army for the occupation of her farm during the war.

Even though Anne kept a day-to-day diary of events on her home Wilton Hill during the war, her answer to the standard list of questions from the commission were sometimes vague.

Q) At what time did the Union Army first encamp on your farm?
A) I think it was in September 1861.

Her answer on her loyalty is truly a lie. The lies she told were no doubt based on her destitute condition, and her hatred of Yankees for which she probably felt justified in attempting to recoup her loss.

> Q) Were you in favor or opposed to Secession?
> A) I was always in favor of the Union and was very much grieved to believe that it might be broken up. We often boarded Union Officer[s], and constantly cared for and fed sick and wounded Union soldiers. We had a safe guard nearly all of the time, and most of the Union officers were very kind to us.

The front of Anne Frobel's beloved house, "Wilton Hill," circa 1915. *Fairfax County Public Library, Photographic Archives.*

She was, however, truthful as to the details of the Union occupation and her ownership of her farm.

Q) How long did the troops occupy your farm?
A) They occupied it the whole four years of the war and for six month after the surrender, until they were mustered out of service. The whole farm was just as bare as it could be and looked like a road. There was not a green thing left on it.

A side view of the dilapidated "Wilton Hill," circa 1915. *Fairfax County Public Library, Photographic Archives.*

Q) Who owns this farm at the present time?
A) I am the owner of it at this time. I suppose the place has been in the family for more than a hundred years.

Anne Frobel never appeared personally before the commission, giving her answers through an intermediary lawyer. She never admitted her brother was a member of the Confederate army. Her claim, like the majority of those filed by Southerners after the war, was not allowed. The waiting period of hoping for restitution after the war was now over for Anne Frobel. Like the other civilians who had suffered in the county, very few received compensation for their losses during the conflict.

A lonely sentinel still guards the Chain Bridge along the Potomac at Fort Marcy in the twenty-first century. *Charles V. Mauro.*

Old Virginia was gone, and although the war had changed the existence of the white population of Fairfax County forever, noted county author Nan Netherton stated that its white citizens "walked backward into the future, their gaze still fixed on the past they left behind." The slaves, however, whose existence had been the predominate cause of the war, were now taking their first steps on the road of freedom, secured by the four most tumultuous years in Fairfax County's—as well as the country's—history.[296]

NOTES

INTRODUCTION

1. Maris A. Vinovskis, *Toward A Social History of the American Civil War, Exploratory Essays* (Cambridge: Cambridge University Press, 1990), 3.

2. Ibid., 12.

3. Juanita Leisch, *An Introduction to Civil War Civilians* (Gettysburg, PA: Thomas Publications, 1994), 1.

4. Ibid., 2.

5. Ibid., 9.

6. Ibid., 27.

7. Ibid., 50.

8. Vinovskis, *Toward a Social History*, 8.

FAIRFAX COUNTY, VIRGINIA

9. Edmund S. Morgan, *American Slavery, American Freedom* (New York: W.W. Norton, 1975), 110.

10. Ibid.; Nan Netherton et al., *Fairfax County, Virginia: A History* (Fairfax: Fairfax County Board of Supervisors, 1992), 5–11; Bradley E. Gernand and Nan Netherton, *Falls Church, A Virginia Village Revisited* (Falls Church, VA: Donning Company/Publishers, 2000), 14; Morgan, *American Slavery*, 196.

11. Robert M. Moxhan, *Annandale, Virginia: A Brief History* (Fairfax: Fairfax County History Commission, 1992), 2; Ellen Anderson, *Salona, Fairfax County Virginia* (Fairfax: Fairfax County Office of Comprehensive Planning, 1979), 1; Charles Preston Poland Jr., *Dunbarton, Dranesville, Virginia* (Fairfax: Fairfax County Office of Comprehensive Planning, 1982), viii; Netherton et al., *Fairfax County*, 15.

12. Ross D. Netherton and Ruby Waldeck, *The Fairfax County Courthouse* (Fairfax County Office of Comprehensive Planning, 1977), 3–5; Fairfax Harrison, *Landmarks of Old Prince William, Volumes I & II* (The Prince William County Historical Commission, Baltimore, MD: Gateway Press, 1987), 321.

13. Netherton and Waldeck, *Fairfax County Courthouse*, 7, 9, 14.

14. Morgan, *American Slavery*, 45.

15. Ibid., 46, 73, 84–85.

16. Ibid., 105, 297, 299.

17. Ibid., 126, 129, 133, 143.

18. Ibid., 204, 299.

19. Bruce Chadwick, *Traveling the Underground Railroad: A Visitor's Guide to More Than 300 Sites* (Secaucus, NJ: Citadel Press Book, 1999), 14; Morgan, *American Slavery*, 301; Netherton et al., *Fairfax County*, 22, 30.

20. Morgan, *American Slavery*, 6.

21. Ibid.

22. Netherton et al., *Fairfax County*, 153

23. Ibid., 154, 156.

24. Ibid., 159, 163; Chalky Gillingham, *The Journal of Chalky Gillingham, Friend in the Midst of Civil War* (Alexandria, VA: Alexandria Monthly Meeting, 1989), 1.

25. Martin Petersilia and Russell Wright, *Hope Park and the Hope Park Mill* (Fairfax County Office of Comprehensive Planning, 1992), 2.

26. Petersilia and Wright, *Hope Park*, 69; Herbert H. Harwood Jr., *Rails to the Blue Ridge: The Washington and Old Dominion Railroad, 1847–1968* (Fairfax Station: Northern Virginia Regional Park Authority, 2000), 13.

27. Petersilia and Wright, *Hope Park*, 72; Ernest B. Furgurson, *Freedom Rising: Washington in the Civil War* (New York: Alfred A. Knopf, 2004), 99.

28. Ibid., *Hope Park*, 72–73.

29. Ibid., 73.

30. James G. Barber, *Alexandria in the Civil War* (M.E. Howard, Inc., 1988), 1.

SECESSION

31. James M. McPherson, *Battle Cry of Freedom: The Civil War Era* (New York: Oxford University Press, 1988), 231; Netherton et al., *Fairfax County*, 315.

32. Brian A. Conley, *Fractured Land: Fairfax County's Roles in the Vote for Secession, May 23, 1861* (Fairfax County: Fairfax County Public Library, 2001),

33. Barber, *Alexandria*, 1.

34. Ibid., 2; Netherton et al., *Fairfax County*, 315.

35. Barber, *Alexandria*, 2; McPherson, *Battle Cry*, 20, 65.

36. Barber, *Alexandria*, 2, 8; Conley, *Fractured Land*, 8; Netherton et al., *Fairfax County*, 315.

37. Netherton et al., *Fairfax County*, 315; Conley, *Fractured Land*, 6–7.

38. Barber, *Alexandria*, 5.

39. Netherton et al., *Fairfax County*, 316; Conley, *Fractured Land*, 6–7.

40. Conley, *Fractured Land*, 8, 35.

41. John W. Deavers, claim #14,841, July 12, 1872, Southern Claims Commission Case Files 1877–1883, Records of the General Accounting Office, 3rd Auditor's Office, Record Group #217, Claims Disallowed by the Commissioners of the Southern Claims Commission, Records of the House of Representatives 1871–1880, Record Group #233, Case Files for Congressional Cases 1884–1952, Records of the U.S. Court of Claims, Record Group #123, National Archives.

42. Conley, *Fractured Land*, 31.

THE ARMIES ARRIVE

43. Barber, *Alexandria*, 7–8.

44. Ibid., 8, 11; Gillingham, *Journal*, 3.

45. Benjamin Franklin Cooling III, *Symbol, Sword and Shield: Defending Washington During the Civil War* (Shippensburg, PA: White Mane Publishing Company, 1991), 35–36.

46. Edgar Warfield, *Manassas to Appomattox: The Civil War Memoirs of Pvt. Edgar Warfield, 17th Virginia Infantry* (McLean, VA: EPM Publications, 1996), 32.

47. Barber, *Alexandria*, 38.

48. Anne S. Frobel, *The Civil War Diary of Anne S. Frobel of Wilton Hill in Virginia* (McLean, VA: EPM Publications, 1992), 17.

49. Barber, *Alexandria*, 16.

50. Ibid., 16; Frobel, *Diary*, 18.

51. Petersilia and Wright, *Hope Park*, 79–80, 84; Gillingham, *Journal*, 4.

52. Barber, *Alexandria*, 38.

53. Ibid., 40–41.

54. Netherton and Waldeck, *Fairfax County Courthouse*, 33.

55. Gernand, *Falls Church*, 35–36.

56. Frobel, *Diary*, 24–25.

57. Warfield, *Memoirs*, 43; Gernand, *Falls Church*, 41.

58. James P. Gannon, *Irish Rebels, Confederate Tigers: A History of the 6th Louisiana Volunteers, 1861–1865* (Campbell, CA: Savas Publishing Company, 1998), 2; John Hennessy, *The First Battle of Manassas, An End To Innocence: July 18–21, 1861* (Lynchburg, VA: H.E. Howard, 1989), 5.

59. Gernand, *Falls Church*, 56; G.G. Benedict, *Vermont In The Civil War, A History Of The Past, Taken By The Vermont Soldiers and Sailors In the War for The Union 1861–5, Volume 1* (Burlington, VT: Free Press Association, 1886), 68–69.

60. Moxhan, *Annandale*, 44–45.

61. Ibid., 42–44; Hennessey, *First Battle of Manassas*, 7–9.

62. Frobel, *Diary*, 48.

63. Jeffrey D. Wert, *General James Longstreet: The Confederacy's Most Controversial Soldier* (New York: Simon & Schuster, 1993), 78.

64. Gernand, *Falls Church*, 60, 62.

65. John S. Mosby, *The Memoirs of Colonel John S. Mosby* (Nashville, TN: J.S. Sanders & Company, 1995), 50; Gernand, *Falls Church*, 69; Wert, *Longstreet*, 81.

66. Cooling, *Symbol, Sword and Shield*, 55, 57, 63; Benjamin Franklin Cooling III and Walton H. Owen II, *Mr. Lincoln's Forts: A Guide to the Civil War Defenses of Washington* (Shippensburg, PA: White Mane Publishing Company, 1988), 30.

67. Gernand, *Falls Church*, 62; Donald C. Hakenson, "This Forgotten Land: A Tour of Civil War Sites and Other Historical Landmarks South of Alexandria, Virginia" (Alexandria, VA: self-published, 2002), 65.

68. Benedict, *Vermont In The Civil War*, 92; Gernand, *Falls Church*, 86–87, 95.

69. Netherton and Waldeck, *Fairfax County Courthouse*, 34; Benedict, *Vermont In The Civil War*, 92, 132–3.

70. William C. Oates, *The War Between the Union and the Confederacy and Its Lost Opportunities* (Dayton, OH: Morningside Bookshop, 1985), 65; Wert, *Longstreet*, 90–91.

71. Cooling, *Symbol, Sword and Shield*, 83.

72. Oates, *War Between the Union and the Confederacy*, 66; Richard L. Korink, *Centreville Historic District* (Fairfax County: Office of Comprehensive Planning, 1984) 8.

73. Ann M. Coleman, claim #9,989, March 7, 1900.

74. Anna Maria Fitzhugh, claim #14,013, January 3, 1873.

75. Emory M. Thomas, *Robert E. Lee: A Biography* (New York: W.W. Norton, 1995), 188–9.

76. Ibid., 195.

77. Conley, *Fractured Land*, 54; James S. Purdy, claim #6,714, January 8, 1867.

78. Ambrose Cock Jr., claim #2,010, November 2, 1871; Moxhan, *Annandale*, 46.

79. James S. Purdy, claim #6,714, January 8, 1867.

80. Cooling and Owen, *Mr. Lincoln's Forts*, 60.

81. Court H. Johnson, claim #17,126, April 6, 1875.

82. Thomas Pulman, claim #18,059, August 9, 1873.

83. John A. Fairfax, claim #2,449 (combined with #12,314), March 3, 1908.

84. James Coleman, claim #14,263, November 23, 1909.

85. Frobel, *Diary*, 21.

86. Mary A. Gossom, claim #2,945, May 21, 1871.

87. Robert T. Scisson, claim #1,680, May 27, 1871.

88. Conley, *Fractured Land*, 63.

89. Daniel Collins, claim #21,391, September 20, 1875.

90. Charles Kirby, claim #12,332, March 10, 1906.

91. Conley, *Fractured Land*, 68.

92. Esther J. Ferguson, claim #6,328, April 28, 1877.

93. William Purcell, claim #1,228, December 25, 1871.

94. Glascoe Gaskins, claim #2,359, May 23, 1872.

95. Mark M. Boatner, *The Civil War Dictionary* (New York: Vintage, 1991), 113; Mary E. Burke, claim #8,345, May 22, 1872.

96. Andrew Murtaugh, claim #17,072, May 23, 1877.

97. Frobel, *Diary*, 57.

98. Ibid., 59.

99. Ambrose Barcroft, claim #17,625, May 13, 1875.

100. John J. Hall, claim #610, June 2, 1871.

101. Nancy and Elcom G. Read, claim #19,016, December 17, 1873.

102. Letitia Strother, claim #20,481, February 22, 1879.

103. Henry D. Biggs, claim #724, April 18, 1874.

104. Josiah B. Bowman, claim #19,350, February 26, 1873.

105. Albert Orcutt, claim #12,128, March 6, 1873.

106. Lott W. Crocker, claim #847, May 24, 1871; Conley, *Fractured Land*, 68, 70.

107. Benjamin D. Carpenter, claim #10,173, June 1900.

108. John Gilbert, claim #20, March 31, 1871.

109. Henry Escridge, claim #20,005, September 24, 1874.

110. Susanna Storms for Alonzo Storms, claim #10,526, December 1872.

111. Henry A. Lockwood, claim #20,523, November 10, 1876.

112. Conley, *Fractured Land*, 70; Thomas J. Carper, claim #15,134, September 14, 1874.

113. Kim Bernard Holien, *Battle of Ball's Bluff* (Orange, VA: Publisher's Press), 3.

114. Conley, *Fractured Land*, 70; Aaron Oliver, claim #15,328, June 18, 1877.

115. Perry Elliott, claim #11,016, March 26, 1874.

116. Conley, *Fractured Land*, 68.

117. Martha Corbin Ball, claim #21,061, October 10, 1873.

118. Reuben Ives, claim #287, May 2, 1871.

119. Catherine Ann Minor, claim #3,831, January 17, 1873.

120. Conley, *Fractured Land*, 57.

121. Mary E. Martin, claim #1,837, April 26, 1873.

122. Adam Martin, claim #11,095, July 18, 1872.

123. Conley, *Fractured Land*, 70.

124. William Sherman, claim #22,111, April 25, 1874.

125. John William Lynch, claim #20,351, June 10, 1874.

126. Reuben Ives, claim #287, May 2, 1871.

127. Hugh W. Throckmorton, claim #1,709, March 27, 1871.

128. James E. Murray, claim #257, March 10, 1877.

129. John E. Febrey, claim #1,841, October 31, 1887.

130. Barber, *Alexandria*, 17.

Major Battles

131. Korink, *Centreville Historic District*, 3–5.

132. Ibid., 5–6.

133. Gernand, *Falls Church*, 155–56.

134. Gillingham, *Journal*, 10.

135. Ibid., 10, 37, 40.

136. Barber, *Alexandria*, 23.

137. Frobel, *Diary*, 80.

138. Wert, *Longstreet*, 98.

139. Ibid., 98.

140. Ibid., 99; Cooling, *Symbol, Sword and Shield*, 104.

141. Petersilia and Wright, *Hope Park*, 87, 89.

142. Netherton and Waldeck, *Fairfax County Courthouse*, 34–35.

143. Bruce Catton, *A Stillness at Appomattox* (New York: Pocket Books, 1958), 318–19.

144. Cooling, *Symbol, Sword and Shield*, 106.

145. Benedict, *Vermont In The Civil War*, 161.

146. Gillingham, *Journal*, 15.

147. Anderson, *Salona*, 32.

148. Frobel, *Diary*, 81–82.

149. Ibid., 83.

150. Cooling, *Symbol, Sword and Shield*, 109–10.

151. Ibid., 121; Barber, *Alexandria*, 32.

152. Cooling, *Symbol, Sword and Shield*, 123; Barber, *Alexandria*, 35.

153. John Codman Ropes, *Campaigns Of The Civil War: The Army Under Pope* (1881; repr., Edison, NJ: Castle Books, 2002), 3–4, 60.

154 Ropes, *The Army Under Pope*, 79; Moxhan, *Annandale*, 48; Gillingham, *Friends*, 18; Gernand, *Falls Church*, 166.

155. Charles V. Mauro, *The Battle of Chantilly (Ox Hill): A Monumental Storm* (Fairfax County: Fairfax County History Commission, 2002), 12.

156. Ibid., 15.

157. Ibid., 23.

158. Ibid., 31.

159. Ibid., 37, 41.

160. Ibid., 42.

161. Ibid., 11; Ropes, *The Army Under Pope*, 166.

162. Mauro, *Battle of Chantilly*, 49.

163. Gernand, *Falls Church*, 167.

164. Ibid., 170.

165. Ibid.

166. Talmadge Thorn, claim #19,861, February 28, 1876.

167. Gernand, *Falls Church*, 170; Oates, *War Between the Union and the Confederacy*, 153.

168. Furgurson, *Freedom Rising*, 202–03; Frobel, *Diary*, 103; *Alexandria Gazette*, January 17, 1863, 3, 14.

169. Thomas J. Evans and James M. Moyer, "Mosby Vignettes: Volume 1" (Fairfax City: Privately printed, 1993), 2.

170. Gernand, *Falls Church*, 178.

171. Cooling, *Symbol, Sword and Shield*, 136, 142.

172. Barber, *Alexandria*, 27.

173. Benedict, *Vermont In The Civil War*, 420.

174. Eric Ward, ed., *Army Life in Virginia, The Civil War Letters of George G. Benedict* (Mechanicsburg, PA: Stackpole Books, 2002), 110.

175. Benedict, *Vermont In The Civil War*, 420.

176. Edwin C. Fitzhugh, claim #14,896, June 17, 1872.

177. Robert Strong, claim #1,819, April 12, 1872.

178. Uriah Ferguson, claim #8,742, November 20, 1871.

179. Ambrose Cock, claim #2,011, October 7, 1873.

180. Lucretia C. Merry, claim #22,124, November 28, 1873.

181. Esther J. Ferguson, claim #6,328, June 15, 1878.

182. John Thomas Bushrod, claim #18,271, April 4, 1873.

183. George W. Johnson, claim #19,993, 1875.

184. Harvey J. Peck, claim #15,324, May 14, 1875.

185. Jesse Harris, claim #7,738, February 6, 1872.

186. Obed Harris, claim #7,739, February 2, 1872.

187. Joseph Harris, claim #16,190, March 28, 1877.

188. Betsey Johnson, claim #10,094, March 14, 1876.

189. Andrew Murtaugh, claim #17,072, May 23, 1877.

190. James W. Wells, claim #21,652, October 30, 1875.

191. John E. Febrey, claim #1,841, October 31, 1867.

192. John William Lynch, claim #20,351, June 10, 1874.

193. Reuben Ives, claim #287, May 2, 1871.

194. Walter H. Erwin, claim #17,471, April 10, 1873.

195. Isaac Haynes, claim #12,872, March 5, 1878; John Dougherty, claim #3,223, June 23, 1873.

196. Henry Clevenger, claim #10,171, January 2, 1900.

197. Almond Birch, claim #22,123, June 6, 1877.

198. Charles Kirby, claim #12,332, March 10, 1906.

199. William and Louisa Ferguson, claim #19,994, December 16, 1873.

200. John W. Elgin, claim #8,991, September 2, 1892.

201. Charles V. Mauro, *Herndon: A Town And Its History* (Charleston, SC: The History Press, 2004), 70; Wesley Hall, claim #14,250, October 1872.

202. Samual T. Brown, claim #12,141, April 23, 1872.

203. Nancy Worster, claim #9,702, April 3, 1900.

204. George W. Steele, claim #9,537, June 5, 1874; Conley, *Fractured Land*, 7.

205. Netherton et al., *Fairfax*, 347.

206. William M. Holsapple, claim #12,693, October 30, 1877.

Guerilla Warfare

207. Moxhan, *Annandale*, 49.

208. Ibid.

209. Alexander Hunter, *The Women of the Debatable Land* (Port Washington, NY: Kennikat Press, 1972), 51.

210. Hugh C. Keen and Horace Mewborn, *43rd Battalion, Virginia Cavalry, Mosby's Command* (Lynchburg, VA: M.E. Howard, 1993), 20, 25, 26.

211. Ibid., 26.

212. John Bakeless, *Spies of the Confederacy* (Mineola, NY: Dover Publications, 1970), 63.

213. Near the Marriott Hotel at the intersection of Centreville Road and the Dulles Toll Road. Evans and Moyer, "Mosby Vignettes," 44.

214. Keen and Mewborn, *43rd Battalion*, 26; Bakeless, *Spies*, 63.

215. Virgil Carrington Jones, *Ranger Mosby* (Chapel Hill: The University of North Carolina Press, 1944), 82; Keen and Mewborn, *43rd Battalion*, 26.

216. John Singleton Mosby, *Mosby's War Reminiscences and Stuart's Cavalry Campaigns* (New York: Pageant Book Company, 1958), 63–67.

217. Mrs. J.M. McWhorter, "Caring for the Soldiers in the Sixties," *Confederate Veteran* 39, nos. 11–12 (November–December 1921), 411.

218. Barber, *Alexandria*, 88–89.

219. Cooling, *Symbol, Sword, and Shield*, 142, 150–51.

220. Netherton, et al., *Fairfax County*, 355; Evans and Moyer, "Mosby Vignettes: Volume 1," 7.

221. Furgurson, *Freedom Rising*, 231.

222. Ibid., 230, 232.

223. Gillingham, *Journal*, 20.

224. Benedict, *Vermont In The Civil War*, 583.

225. This sawmill is believed to have been located within sight of the station, just west on Elden Street based on the G.M. Hopkins *Atlas of Fifteen Miles Around Washington Including Fairfax and Alexandria Counties* (Fairfax: Fairfax County History Commission, Office of Comprehensive Planning, November 1986). The map shows a steam sawmill on the 1878 map. A used car lot currently occupies this location. See also Benedict, *Vermont In The Civil War*, 584; Keen and Mewborn, *43rd Battalion*, 39–40.

226. Benedict, *Vermont In The Civil War*, 584.

227. The Hannah House was located at 727 Elden Street across from the railroad station and was also known as the Printz House, purchased by Raymond Printz in 1938. It is currently the site of the Mainstreet Bank at 727 Elden Street. The Purdie house was on the site of the home of Mrs. R.C. Printz. Evans and Moyer, "Mosby Vignettes," 44; Virginia Carter Castleman, *Reminiscences of an Oldest Inhabitant, A Nineteenth Century Chronicle* (Herndon, VA: The Herndon Historical Society, 1976), 38; Keen and Mewborn, *43rd Battalion*, 40; Elizabeth Ellmore, *History of Herndon: The Herndon Observer's Neighbor to Neighbor Cookbook*, compiled by Anne Ward Crocker, (Herndon, VA: The Herndon Publishing Co., 1982), 99.

228. Mosby, *War Reminiscences*, 71–72.

229. Castleman, *Reminiscences*, 27–29.

230. Frobel, *Diary*, 170.

231. Barber, *Alexandria*, 90–91.

232. William Holland, claim #17,091, April 5, 1877.

233. John F. Webb, claim #1,363, June 16, 1871.

234. James Coleman, claim #14,263, November 23, 1909.

235. Barber, *Alexandria*, 91; Frobel, *Diary*, 196.

236. Ibid., 204.

237. Gillingham, *Journal*, 20.

238. Sanford W. Cooksey, claim #5,382, May 22, 1872; Uriah Ferguson, claim #8,742, November 20, 1871; Charles W. Kitchen, claim #13,977, March 8, 1873.

239. Benjamin Lewis, claim #21,737, May 31, 1877.

240. Robert T. Scisson, claim #1,680, May 27, 1871.

241. Mason Shipman, claim #16,637, June 2, 1871.

242. Frobel, *Diary*, 206–07.

ATTACKS ON WASHINGTON, FALLS CHURCH AND ANNANDALE

243. Cooling, *Symbol, Sword and Shield*, 181.

244. Ibid., 193.

245. Ibid., 198.

246. Ibid., 204–06.

247. Ibid., 209, 213, 222, 225.

248. Barber, *Alexandria*, 95.

249. Gillingham, *Journal*, 22.

250. Ibid., 269–70; Gernand, *Falls Church*, 201–02.

251. Ibid., 204.

252. Moxham, *Annandale*, 49–50.

253. Ibid., 50–51.

254. Gernand, *Falls Church*, 216; Frobel, *Diary*, 215.

255. John R. Bigelow, claim #1,125, May 26, 1871.

256. Conley, *Fractured Land*, 73.

257. James W. Green, claim #18,595, November 17, 1873.

Final Review

258. Cooling, *Symbol, Sword and Shield*, 225–26.

259. Ibid., 226.

260. Ibid., 232.

261. Ibid., 236.

262. Ibid., 238.

263. Gillingham, *Journal*, 25.

264. Barber, *Alexandria*, 101.

265. Ibid., 102.

266. Frobel, *Diary*, 247–48.

267. James S. Purdy, claim #6,714, January 8, 1867.

268. William S. Reid, claim #18,060, February 15, 1873.

269. John Dean, claim #2,009, June 1, 1871.

270. John Haislip, claim #14,555, June 8, 1877.

271. Mary A. Gossom, claim #2,945, May 21, 1871.

272. Gernand, *Falls Church*, 217.

273. Phyllis Pearson, claim #9,241, January 11, 1897.

274. John Jackson, claim #19,246, February 25, 1873.

275. Joseph H. Cockrell, claim #21,735, July 19, 1877.

276. Lewis Bailey, claim #1,291, June 15, 1871.

277. George Brice, claim #8,645, October 18, 1871; William Y. Dulin, claim #14,239, December 11, 1907.

278. Ambrose Barcroft, claim #17,625, May 13, 1875.

279. Conley, *Fractured Land*, 69; Joseph Sewell, claim #13,813, April 25, 1873.

280. Samuel Sharper, claim #10,700, October 14, 1874.

281. Archibald Merchant, claim #15,880, February 4, 1875.

282. James McWilliams, claim #14,926, July 22, 1972.

283. William C. Lipscomb, claim #21,716, February 18, 1879.

284. Charlotte E. Read, claim #12,956, n.d.

AFTERMATH AND SUMMARY OF CLAIMS

285. Andrew M.D. Wolf, "Black Settlement in Fairfax County: Virginia During Reconstruction" (Preliminary Draft, December 1975), 20.

286. Netherton et al., *Fairfax County*, 373.

287. *Gazette*, October 20, 1865.

288. Wolf, "Black Settlement in Fairfax County," 18.

289. Netherton et al., *Fairfax County*, 381.

290. Brian A. Conley, *Return To Union, Fairfax County's Role in the Adoption of the Virginia's Constitution of 1870* (Fairfax County: Fairfax County Public Library, 2001), 8.

291. Conley, *Return to Union*, 8, 10.

292. Moxhan, *Annandale*, 58.

293. Ibid., 61.

294. Barber, *Alexandria*, 102.

295. Gillingham, *Journal*, 34–35.

296. Netherton et al., *Fairfax County*, 389.

INDEX

ABOUT THE AUTHOR

Mr. Mauro is the author and photographer of *Herndon: A Town and Its History*, *Herndon: A History in Images* and *The Battle of Chantilly (Ox Hill): A Monumental Storm*, for which he received the Nan Netherton Heritage Award for his historical research, writing and photography. He is also the writer and co-producer of the independent film *The Battle of Chantilly (Ox Hill)*, based on his book.

Chuck is a past president of the Herndon Historical Society and is a member of the Historic Centreville Society, Ltd., the Bull Run and Capital Hill Civil War Round Tables, the Friends of Fort Ward, the Louisiana Historical Association Memorial Hall Foundation, Inc., the National Center for Civil War Photography and the Civil War Preservation Trust. He is also a member and past president of the Manassas Warrenton Camera Club and has won numerous prizes for his photography.

Mr. Mauro received a Bachelor of Science from the University of Maryland and a Masters in Business Administration from Temple University. He is currently a manager at the Federal Aviation Administration (FAA).

He lives with his wife in Herndon, Virginia.

Please visit us at
www.historypress.net